Charismatic to the core

A fresh approach to authentic leadership

Nikki Owen

Dear reader,

I want to give you a refreshingly different perspective to an attribute that has tantalised and fascinated people for centuries. Written for leaders, including aspiring leaders working within a commercial environment, this book is designed to help you to develop more of your natural charisma and support the vast array of benefits an organisation can access when they open up to the value gained from nurturing this powerful attribute within their leadership team.

Nikki Owen

Charismatic to the Core

A fresh approach to authentic leadership

© Nikki Owen

ISBN 978-1-909116-48-1

eISBN 978-1-909116-49-8

Designed & Published in 2015 by SRA Books

The right of Nikki Owen to be identified as the author
of this work has been asserted by her in accordance
with the Copyright, Designs and Patents Act 1988.

A CIP record of this book is available from the British Library.

Printed in the UK by TJ International, Padstow.

This book is dedicated to Mr Addezio.
Your charisma in court on the 22nd December 1978 inspired
my lifelong passion. You created legal history and set me on my path.

Contents

Acknowledgements

I am deeply indebted to a number of people who have made a contribution to this book which is the legacy of my life's work.

Sue Skinner, you are an inspiration. You believed in me when my vision was simply jumbled thoughts inside my head. You continue to support me with your wisdom, guidance and vast expertise. I love our friendship.

Mark Wharton, you listened to me patiently for hours as I talked through my processes. At the very beginning when I was plagued with self-doubt you quoted from *The Field of Dreams* – 'If you build it they will come.' These words gave me courage to just go for it.

Frank Bastow and Andy Mildner, you guided me towards an absolute knowing of my brand and my target audience. Down-to-earth, kind and very direct – your observations resonate deeply with me.

Alan Westbury, you read my draft book six times and offered feedback from the perspective of a logical business leader. Thank you for your time and insights.

Paul Webb, from the first time we met for a *Daily Mail* shoot your photography has been breathtaking. Thank you for taking such natural photos of me for this book and for being such an important part of the team when I delivered my charisma seminars at The Globe.

Les Greve, you worked tirelessly on my energy. From my own personal experience I know your approach works!

Corah Clark my soul sister, you have enhanced my charisma programmes with your wisdom, intuition and patience. I feel blessed to have met you.

Rose Bolam, my wonderful daughter who has laughed and cried with me. You are the love of my life and I am so proud of the woman you have become. It can't have been easy living with me at times, particularly during my frenetic writing phase.

To all the people I have worked with over the years, particularly the early adopters who asked me to work with their leadership teams. To my clients who have trusted and believed in me – I continue to feel in awe of your courage. This book could not have been written without you.

Foreword

My very first meeting with Nikki several years ago was serendipitous! I had heard that there was this amazing woman, doing amazing things with leaders working with energy. My own purpose and passion is 'to catalyse continuous breakthrough in our lives as leaders and the wider systems we touch.' I will do anything to take myself and my members to new places of awareness, so Nikki's name had gone into my rolling action list with the imperative 'source contact details and invite to lead one of my CEO circles.' That very morning, I was meeting a client at a London Club and I was introduced to one Nikki Owen who just happened to be finishing a meeting of her own. I knew then that the concept of 'what we think about we attract into our lives' had some validity. Our connection was instantaneous.

My CEO group loved the rather shocking, provocative and edgy session. The ideas presented by Nikki on her model of charisma and working with energy states challenged their long established beliefs and models of the world. Wow, this is exactly what all of us need in our uncertain world today. If all leaders can move effortlessly from the mindset of the 'knower' to the 'learner' then the world opens up to unlimited possibilities! I loved the new belief we adopted from this session, 'Just because my mind can't understand it, it doesn't mean it's not possible!' This is where all breakthroughs occur. Nikki certainly became an awakener of possibility for us that day!

Nikki Owen wrote this book specifically for me; she also wrote this book for each one of us who are wanting to explore our edges, continuously raise our consciousness and allow our light to shine even brighter. Her passion and purpose aligns with all of us who want to lead more conscious and authentic lives. This special book, for me, is a synthesis, a distillation, a resource handbook, of the many theories, principles and concepts that have guided my own life and work over the years. Particularly in the first six chapters there is an absolute goldmine of nuggets of wisdom, handed down from wisdom teachers, scientists, therapists and eminent thinkers that are crystallized into pragmatic and inspiring transformation insights and activities born out of rigour and validation.

Then from Chapter 7, we move into the 'bonkers' world of dowsing, chakra balancing, channelling with dead masters, screaming hatred at an apple to see what happens! Why do I love this so much? For me I am liberated by Nikki's passion to pilot, experiment and challenge. She takes the science, the known, and integrates philosophy, psychology, spirituality, cosmology and more and leads us beyond the realms of 'knowing' to experiencing and trusting in 'not knowing'. It is in the 'not knowing' that we can unlock our huge potential and our authentic state. When we step into judgements and criticism then we close down to compassion and possibility. The work she has been pioneering, sometimes contentiously, for years is now becoming acknowledged and seriously validated.

The past ten years have seen an explosion of 'how to' books but often they result in little more than 'that's interesting'. For me, what is missing, most fundamentally, is a deep understanding of what it means to cultivate and activate those human capabilities which determine whether any significant change ever gets implemented. This is the great value of Nikki's work and writing in this book. Charisma or authentic mastery begins with mastery of the self, at the emotional level, a mental level born from a strong sense of ethics and a spiritual level. Anything more than that is not needed.

I was one of the CEOs who was triggered initially by the word 'charisma'. I had read the literature which stated that it could even be dangerous in a leader, and then alternatively that if you didn't have some charisma which implied a larger than life personality, you would be doomed in your career; an aspect I instantly resisted, believing that everyone had the potential to shine in different ways. For me charisma was quite a contentious word… until I met Nikki.

Her definition of 'charisma' as an authentic power that captivates the hearts and minds of others just feels so resonant. How can we let our lights shine more brightly?

Charisma for me in this special book is a unifying word and a gateway to understanding the universal principles of our existence and our futility in trying to swim upstream. Nikki reminds us that charismatic leadership is not a skill but a deep reconnection with who we are at our core. We are all just strands of pulsating energy connecting everything into a unified field, but charismatic leaders appear to be deeply connected to systems bigger than themselves.

I have often called Nikki an 'edgewalker'. No one ever has been transformed by remaining safely in our comfort zone of knowingness. We owe it to the world to keep pushing our boundaries and to continuously evolve to ever higher levels of consciousness.

Nikki is a living example of what she preaches, a woman of sensitivity, impeccability and keen consciousness. It is not just this comment that makes her a special human being, or more successful as a business person, or as an amazing teacher, or a wonderful mum… but that it makes her a special human being who I am proud to call a friend. I highly recommend that you take this powerful journey with Nikki, learning to transform, mind, body and spirit. As you explore these concepts with openness and curiosity, neither you nor the world will be the same!

Thank goodness!

Sue Cheshire
Founder Global Leaders Academy

Introduction

There are defining moments in everyone's life that causes them to choose a path that feels meaningful and potent with possibilities. My moment happened on 22 December 1978, in Court 13 at the Old Bailey when, at the age of 18, I faced the real and frightening probability of spending 12 to 15 years in Holloway Prison. My barrister, Mr Addezio, defended me in a case that made legal history. Despite all the precedents, Mr Addezio presented a compelling argument that convinced the judge that I was no longer a threat to society and I walked free. I had just witnessed, just experienced one man's charisma and how he had in that moment, transformed my own life against all odds. That's when my lifelong fascination with charisma began.

My journey to the woman I am today has not been an easy one, yet my purpose in life was awakened by this dramatic incident. I have learned courage and resilience in the face of those who told me that my work on charisma would never be accepted, let alone appreciated by the world's corporate leaders. Today I am a successful, award winning speaker on charisma, teaching business leaders how to connect with the essence of who they truly are at their core. Whilst many of these leaders are initially surprised by my approach, those people who have benefited from working with me have experienced a dramatic shift in their ability to transform and engage others.

This book is the legacy of 35 years of personal and professional development. As the eldest child of three from a happy and middle class home I was often described as a good little girl, exceptionally polite, a bit shy and always eager to please and help my parents. Growing up I learned how to dance and as I entered my teens I was approached to do part-time modelling work. A model child in a model family with a bright and golden future ahead of me.

Then things began to change as I started to suffer from extreme mood swings and began to eat compulsively. As the weight piled on I became suicidal and committed innumerable bizarre acts of destruction and self-mutilation. I no longer recognised the 'model child' I once was. I felt as if a monster had taken over my mind and my body. My life was set on 'self-destruct'. Tensions at home increased as my anti-social behaviour worsened. At 18, obese and uncontrollable, I was remanded in Holloway Prison for twice setting fire to my family home, the second time with intent to kill.

Because I was so violent I was incarcerated in solitary confinement where I was fed through a hatch in the door. I was issued with a dress made out of indestructible material so I couldn't hang myself and the cell was kept in darkness.

My parents could not understand why their perfectly normal daughter had suddenly turned into a raving lunatic and so they approached eight of the UK's top psychiatrists and asked them to examine me and give an expert opinion whilst I was in Holloway Prison. Each psychiatric report was bleak and damning. I was described as 'a maniacal psychopath, incurably insane and a danger to society'. As a result of their reports an application was made for me to go to Broadmoor, the high security psychiatric hospital for the criminally insane. In desperation my parents went to meet one of these psychiatrists to try to understand what had caused my apparent madness. It was during one of these meetings that my father learned about the endocrine system and hormones.

In a frantic race against time my parents researched cases of women whose menstrual periods had caused the onset of bizarre mood swings. This led them to Dr Katrina Dalton, an endocrinologist and expert in premenstrual syndrome. PMS is the recurrence of diverse symptoms, including asthma, epilepsy, sinusitis and psychological changes, which occur a few days before menstruation starts, followed by normality once bleeding has ceased. Dr Dalton agreed to examine me in prison and her report stated that my case was a clear example of PMS due to a hormonal imbalance. I was immediately taken off the massive doses of sedatives I had been prescribed to keep me docile and was given hormone treatment based on blood tests that showed low progesterone levels.

Within three weeks of taking this treatment, my behaviour had improved and I was allowed out of solitary confinement. My parents decided to ask the same psychiatrists to re-examine me and each of their reports referred to my 'miraculous' recovery. When my case finally went to trial, the prosecution was delayed in traffic giving Judge Morris the opportunity to review all of the reports in great detail. His judgement was historic and unprecedented. It was the first time in legal history that PMS was used and accepted as a mitigating factor as part of the defence.

My case attracted a media frenzy at the time. Although I was a free woman, my life was in tatters. The emotional guilt about the hurt and worry I had caused my family was hard to live with and I held a bitter hatred towards myself for my 'evil' actions. I had spiralled into the depths of despair and believed I was worthless. Life was too painful, too fraught and too lonely. In prison I wrote long and lengthy letters to my dad and on one occasion asked him, 'Dad, if God exists why am I going through all this?' My dad responded with words of such great significance that they remain etched in my heart:

> Nicola, if there wasn't ugliness in the world, how would you know beauty? If there wasn't sickness how would you appreciate good health? If we don't experience bad times how will we ever appreciate the good times? One day Nicola you'll look back on this time and realise why you are going through what you are experiencing because this time will pass and define the woman you are destined to become.

Looking back I realise that my own suffering and pain in my teens taught me compassion, courage and resilience. I learned that in my darkest moments there is always a message of hope, a kind gesture that nourishes and shapes our character.

So my path was set when I was 18. Mr Addezio triggered a lifelong fascination with charisma, one that has culminated in helping thousands of business leaders to become more charismatic. The traumatic experiences I had endured as a teenager caused me to make a promise to myself that I have never broken: to be true to who I really am. Today, I allow the real authentic me to guide my decisions and actions around all aspects of my life and in all contexts. Having survived a deeply disturbing set of circumstances I became aware of a deep awakening that caused me to question the meaning of what I had gone through. I felt a growing need to make sense out of what had happened to me. As I accepted that there is always a gift in every trauma, I began to change the way I interacted with people and my approach to life altered significantly. This approach has shaped the woman I am today. Mr Addezio's charisma changed my life and triggered my potential, potential that I had no idea I possessed. I will always remember the spark of inspiration he ignited within me that day.

Charisma is tough to define

Bill Clinton, Winston Churchill, Eva Peron, Princess Diana, Nelson Mandela, Dr Martin Luther King. Six ordinary people with a great gift – when they spoke, millions listened in awe – when they walked, millions followed. Six people, one theme – charisma. According to *Harvard Business Review* and the University of Lausanne, charismatic leaders outperform their non-charismatic peers by 60 per cent. Many great leaders have invested time and energy into cultivating this powerful attribute: the ability to hold others in the palm of their hands. People have different perceptions about who is charismatic and many of those leaders most frequently cited as being charismatic have diverse personalities. This makes 'charisma' tough to define. If you can't define it, then how can you begin to develop it within yourself? Are you comfortable with the thought of becoming more charismatic or do you believe that if you develop your charisma you will compromise your ability to be genuine and authentic? Any concerns that you may have are shared by many shareholders of large corporations who believe that powerful charismatic leaders with the ability to inspire followers may lead their business into reckless and potentially damaging situations.

Learning from charismatic icons

Initially, as I began studying charismatic icons, I realised that each icon expressed their charisma differently. This presented a challenge. If you want to learn a new skill, then you model the behaviours of an individual who demonstrates excellence in this skill. If each charismatic icon demonstrates charisma in a unique way, then how can it be taught to others using traditional leadership development tools?

Global research

In 2003 I was given an opportunity to conduct a piece of global research with Vic Conant, President of the Nightingale-Conant Corporation, who are world leaders in self-development. Our research with 2,663 organisations concentrated on identifying the barriers that prevent sustainable sales growth. The barrier that leaders find hardest to resolve is negative mindset. This light bulb moment showed me that when it came to developing charisma I had been looking in the wrong direction. If you try to adopt a charismatic behaviour, posture or gesture that is out of alignment with who you really are, at your core, then you unwittingly convey a lack of authenticity when you communicate. This immediately blocks your natural charisma.

Throwing away the rule book

I discarded many of the traditional leadership development tools and began searching for methods and techniques that worked from an 'inside-out' perspective. I wanted to explore the principle that if an individual feels and sees their core self as charismatic, do they naturally express their unique blend of charisma with a unique blend of behaviours? Was it possible that more introverted personality types could develop charisma and does everyone have an innate ability to become more charismatic? I intuitively felt that charisma could only be understood if explored from a less orthodox perspective. I became fascinated by the tiny and rebellious world of quantum mechanics where the logical laws of physics are turned upside down. Dr Bruce Lipton inspired my interest in cellular biology and epigenetics – the study of how environment and emotions determine the way genes in our body are activated and expressed. When my autobiography was published in the early 1990s, a chance meeting with hypnotist, Paul McKenna, during a televised interview on the *Richard and Judy* show, led me into the world of neurolinguistic programming and hypnosis.

Noetic science

My appetite for powerful tools that work at a deep level became insatiable. I became an accomplished dowser, gained accreditation as a Reiki Master, and trained with Tad James in California in Time Line Therapy techniques. I explored the meridians used within traditional Chinese medicine and became an advanced practitioner in Emotional Freedom Techniques. After studying and using Kirlian photography to better understand the link between energy and charisma, I learned Matrix Reimprinting with Karl Dawson, which proved to be another intriguing doorway to building more personal impact. I got my feet burned in Portugal when I qualified as a firewalking instructor (never again!) – although this did teach me an invaluable lesson around the power of our belief systems. Then, former astronaut, Edgar Mitchell's work on human potential and extended human capabilities caught my attention because of the extraordinary work he was doing at the Institute of Noetic Sciences. My intuition was heightened when I began attending a weekly psychic circle with the gifted medium, Paul Wayman, who helped me to attain exceptionally high levels of sensory awareness and emotional intelligence. My newly acquired perception landed me a series of small projects as a political commentator when I freely shared my views about the 'real person' behind 'the politician' based on subtle as well as not so subtle non-verbal indicators. My heightened sensory awareness has been a big hit in the corporate world because leaders are astonished with how much I am able to know about them based on their energy.

A metaphor using apples

As the connection between charisma, engagement and followship became clearer, I realised that leaders were generally unaware about the extent to which their thoughts and emotions impact on their physical reality. So I created my own controversial experiment using apples – the Big Apple Experiment™ – that captured the media's attention, not all of it in a good way. This demonstrates that negative thinking and focused intent causes disengagement, ill health (due to a suppressed immune system), damage in relationships, insecurity, low self-esteem and stress. Apples became my visual metaphor to show how people are affected by their emotions, at home and at work. I discovered that the quickest and cheapest antidote to what I coined the Rotten Apple Syndrome was charisma, administered either directly from another individual (charismatic leadership) or from individuals themselves (increased charismatic presence).

Testing at the Globe Theatre

In 2008 I launched my charisma blueprint that guaranteed to transform an individual's charisma in just two days and began running regular seminars for corporate leaders at Shakespeare's Globe Theatre. This gave me the opportunity to test the efficacy of my methods over a five year period. As my reputation for developing charisma began to build, I was invited to run charisma masterclasses for CEO groups, who were renowned for being tough and uncompromising and who had a preference for facts, statistics and traditional leadership processes. After initial scepticism, demand for my controversial charisma talks and keynote speeches continued to grow as business leaders from all types of industries appeared open and genuinely interested in my spiritual approach to developing their charisma. Over a two year period I won a variety of awards and started to work internationally. In 2012, I launched the Charisma Model Programme to FTSE 500 companies and began measuring the impact of charisma on business performance – giving me further opportunities to acquire more hard evidence and compelling organisational case studies. These early adopters became raving fans of my methods and I started to train people within those organisations with tools that enabled them to promote charisma in a way that was sustainable.

Napoleon Hill's invisible counsellors

Curiosity led me to look at the transcendental qualities that charismatic individuals possess. I was inspired by the deceased American author, Napoleon Hill, who in 1937 first published his iconic bestselling book, *Think and Grow Rich*, based on 20 years of research. (This has subsequently sold millions of copies worldwide). Having read his chapter on the '13th step' I decided to replicate his 'invisible counsellors' process on 26 October 2013. This involved an innovative technique that enabled a small group of intuits to tap into the wisdom of some of the world's most charismatic leaders who were no longer living. I invited a selection of today's business leaders to pose questions and the responses were astonishing.

Treading a new path

In the beginning, even with the impressive results I had gathered from my work at the Globe, my unique approach to charisma was a tough sell. It felt on a par with selling the first ever microwave. Hundreds of people attended my open programmes and described them as life-changing. Despite this, heads of leadership development struggled to gain budget approval to run a pilot programme – it was just too strange, too weird and too unconventional. My beliefs were sorely tested as I kept reminding myself that I was able to make a huge difference to employee engagement, motivation and resilience. I now recognise that every obstacle and setback shaped the next step in my approach. When you are treading a new path, some people fight against it, feeling threatened that their beliefs may be exposed as no longer relevant in today's world. Even though some of the criticisms and insults dented my confidence, there was a greater number of people who believed I was pioneering the ultimate in authentic and inspirational leadership development. Today an increasing number of organisations are prepared to step out of their 'conventional heads' and embrace an exciting new way to empower their leadership teams.

Igniting your charismatic potential

My intention in writing this book is to give you a clear understanding of my methods so you can improve your own charisma in a way that is easy, immediate and feels good. It is crammed with case studies, tips and exercises, giving you the opportunity to put into practice the theory contained on these pages. There may be occasions when my concepts stretch your current belief system. Some of what you read may really resonate with you personally and some chapters may leave you speechless. Packed with roller coaster highs and lows in the pursuit of my life's purpose, I continue to remain driven by the belief that everyone, including you, has the potential to transform, inspire and ignite others to achieve more of what they want. Charisma is not the birthright of the lucky few; it is an attribute that we can all possess.

Are you ready for this?

Chapter 1

———

Someone to follow

Extensive research and numerous studies examining the benefits of charisma confirm that people with high levels of charisma are happier, healthier, enjoy more success in their chosen careers and possess increased resilience to the challenges and difficulties that life presents. If the advantages of charisma are so appealing, why then do the majority of organisations shy away from developing the charismatic potential of their leadership team?

An undesirable attribute

There are people who subscribe to the theory that charisma cannot be taught; you either have it or you don't. Other people perceive charisma as a form of psychological bondage that poses an inherent risk for their organisation. I remember when our business development director had a meeting with a major high street financial institution. During the presentation he was a little surprised when their HR director asked: 'Do we really want charismatic leaders?' Charisma can trigger a strong negative reaction because of the legacy left by disgraced and selfish charismatic leaders. Remember the public outcry about the former CEO of Royal Bank of Scotland, Fred Goodwin? The media publisher, Robert Maxwell?

Even when an organisation's charismatic leader has proved to be an asset to the organisation, what happens to the business after the leader has moved on? How would the public and investors of the Virgin empire react if Richard Branson cut his connection with the Virgin brand? The former CEO of Sainsbury's, Justin King, used his charisma as well as other attributes to create a tripling of profits during his ten year tenure. Yet on the day he resigned almost £400 million was wiped from Sainsbury's share value. Little wonder that corporate competency frameworks rarely feature charisma as a desirable leadership trait.

The dark side of charisma

The corporate prejudice against charisma pales into insignificance when looking at the impact of charisma on a nation when used with evil intent. Historical writer and documentary maker Laurence Rees produced a disturbing three-part series – *The Dark Charisma* – based on Adolf Hitler, an awkward, dysfunctional man who developed a level of charismatic attraction almost without parallel in history. Hitler shows that charisma is highly dangerous when possessed by a megalomaniac. Adolf Hitler was without question an extraordinarily charismatic presenter. Certainly in terms of his rise to power, his personal charisma was one of the most effective tools that he used to tap into the collective psyche of the German people. The *Harvard Business Review* published an interesting view from Dr Tomas Chamorro-Premuzic (2012), international authority in personality profiling and psychometric testing. Dr Premuzic argues that, amongst other things, charisma disguises psychopaths, distracts and destructs, and is responsible for 'downgrading leadership to just another form of entertainment'. Whilst I disagree with much of Dr Premuzic's article, it is well written, and certainly mirrors the distrust that the business community seems to have about charismatic leaders. The sweeping generalisation that some individuals may use their charismatic presence inappropriately often prevents corporations from taking charisma seriously. Whilst I concur that charisma can be used for good or for evil, that distinction need not prevent an individual or their organisation from benefiting from what is a genuine competitive advantage. As with any attribute, there is a mantle of responsibility inherently implied for the charismatic leader.

Charisma increases success

Today most leaders acknowledge that a charismatic leader appears to effortlessly attract loyal and supportive 'followship'. Charismatic leaders attract more publicity and more attention from outside groups, as well as exerting a strong (albeit invisible) bond with their organisation's workforce. Numerous studies and many different credible research sources (CBI, 2014) show that charismatic leaders outperform their non-charismatic peers by an average of 60 per cent.

Charisma improves engagement

There is a proven link between organisational double-digit growth and high engagement levels. A Hay Group Insight Report (Hay Group, 2012) that examined engagement within 1,610 organisations concluded that over the past few years employee engagement levels across the world have declined. This is happening at the very point when organisations really need to deliver better performances than ever and often with less resources due to tough economic trading conditions. More than 44 per cent of the global workforce intends to leave their employer within five years, and more than 21 per cent are intending to leave within two years. These statistics are set against a difficult world economy and depressed job market that must be having a significant impact on reducing employee mobility and churn. Clearly there is now a build-up of restlessness and frustration, which, as the report suggests, is likely to result in a mass staff exodus. A third of employees reported that they are unable to perform optimally, with an average of 33 per cent of workers claiming that barriers put in place by the organisation are preventing them from excelling at work. The behaviours demonstrated by engaged employees are very different to behaviours demonstrated by disengaged employees. Charismatic leaders build higher levels of workforce engagement. In *The Leadership Quarterly* in 2006, Joyce Bono and Remus Ilies used scenario experiments, cross-sectional surveys and laboratory studies to prove that inspirational and charismatic leaders had a stronger emotional effect on employees and gained greater levels of employee cooperation than their non-charismatic counterparts. Charismatic leaders affect both their followers and the organisational culture. This 'mood contagion' means that charismatic leaders are capable of altering workforce attitudes, beliefs and motivation, making changes that are not easily implemented through conventional leadership approaches alone.

Charisma and talent

A 2009 survey that analyses employment trends (Nixon, 2009) revealed that attracting the right talent and skills was one of the biggest challenges for employers over the next decade. Great people want to work for great leaders. The biggest differentiator among the organisations of the future will be the ability to build world-class capability and skills. The war for talent exists at all levels of an organisation and charismatic leaders are more effective at attracting and retaining talent because they naturally create better quality relationships. Mark Carney, the Canadian who took over as the governor of the Bank of England in July 2013, has a movie-star brand of charisma that has seen people's perceptions towards Canadians move from 'zeros to heroes' in the UK. People are now queuing up to work for the trendy and eco-friendly Carney who has transformed the staid Bank of England culture into a genuinely exciting and collaborative place to work.

Charisma and resilience

The belief that leaders have the endless stamina, ideas and skills it takes to deliver success year after year is an old-fashioned fallacy. Today's leaders have to be able to bounce back, cope, renew and revitalise. They need to be tough. They need to be resilient. A passion for excellence can only take leaders so far because they will burn out if their physical, emotional and mental limitations are ignored. A study by Korn Ferry (Nixon, 2009) found that 90 per cent of leaders were 'let go' due to physical or mental conditions that impaired their leadership effectiveness. If organisational changes are planned without consideration of the impact on the human condition, this causes the current leadership to falter and breeds inefficiency in the next crop of leaders. Charismatic leaders possess more natural resilience because they tend to be more authentic and more self-aware. They tend to place more importance on 'heart count' rather than 'head count' efficiency. You can read more about why charisma naturally builds high levels of resilience in Chapter 4.

Charisma and health

When we feel good our brain releases chemicals such as serotonin and oxytocin that perpetuate a feeling of balance, strengthen our immune system and ensure good health. When we feel stressed, our hypothalamus, a tiny region at the base of our brain, sets off an internal alarm system. Cortisol is released into our system and activates our fight or flight response. Cortisol is not supposed to remain in our system for long because it alters immune system responses and suppresses the digestive, reproductive and growth systems. When we experience long-term stress at work our whole system becomes anxious, paranoid and fearful. Our job is then literally killing us. Charismatic people are more accepting of themselves and more accepting of others. This provides the ideal inner emotional landscape for developing our potential, growth, adaptability to change and the qualities of charisma. Because charismatic leaders are more comfortable in their own skin, they operate in a way that supports and nourishes their immune system and consequently their health. As a result charismatic leaders tend to be healthier when compared to their less charismatic peers.

What is charisma?

How can you develop your own charisma without knowing exactly what it is? During general and everyday communication, different words mean different things to different people. Certain phrases trigger a strong emotional response in some people yet not in others. So imagine the variety and scope of meanings people can attribute to something as abstract and intangible as charisma. When I don't understand the meaning of a particular word, a quick look at the online dictionary gives me instant clarity and understanding. So, at first glance, Wikipedia and the Oxford Dictionary both describe charisma as a 'compelling attractiveness or charm that can inspire devotion in others' and 'a divinely conferred power or talent'. As you then start to explore under the surface of what charisma really means, you'll find a multitude of leadership experts, scholars, sociologists, organisational psychotherapists, coaches and gurus who give numerous and contradictory views on defining charisma. In 1947, renowned German sociologist, Max Weber (Eisenstadt, 1968), categorised leadership into three styles and defined the charismatic style as:

> A certain quality of an individual personality, by virtue of which one is 'set apart' from ordinary people and treated as endowed with supernatural, superhuman, or at least specifically exceptional powers or qualities. These as such are not accessible to the ordinary person, but are regarded as divine in origin or as exemplary, and on the basis of them the individual concerned is treated as a leader.

Weber's choice of language is very provocative: 'supernatural', 'superhuman', 'exceptional'. These words immediately place charisma into the scarcity box because how many people do we know who we could describe using those three words? Weber perceived charisma as a set of traits or distinguishing qualities, such as being visionary, energetic, unconventional and exemplary. This view contrasts with studies by Professor of Organisational Behaviour, Robert House, who determined in 1977 that charisma is a set of behaviours. House cited behaviours such as exhibiting high levels of self-confidence, persistence, determination, passion and optimism. More recently, the theory that charisma is created from different component parts or behaviours and can be learned and perfected by anyone is cited by Olivia Fox Cabane in her book, *The Charisma Myth* (2012). In 1995, Fernando Molero, an expert researcher in charisma and transformational leadership, proposed a new classification of charisma, based on Sigmund Freud's psychoanalysis. This stated that 'charisma is the individual's ego, driven by a desire to become a dominant father figure'. Another refreshingly different perspective is offered by Gerry Spence (2008), renowned US trial lawyer, who describes 'charisma as energy from the heart zone'. Dr Tony Alessandra (2000), leadership motivator, plays it safe with his definition that 'charisma is an ability to influence others positively by connecting with them physically, emotionally and intellectually'. The more I searched for a definitive definition of charisma, the more confused I felt. Looking closely at the Robert House/Olivia Fox Cabane definition means that you would need to improve your charisma by developing different charismatic behaviours. Yet what if these charismatic behaviours are not aligned with who you truly are inside? If on the other hand you accept Max Weber's definition, then you have to accept that you either have this 'super power' or it's game over for you on the charisma front.

You don't have to shout or show off

In 2008 Alan Chapman, owner of a free online educational resource 'BusinessBalls', and I ran a competition for six months to encourage business people to submit their own definition of charisma. From the hundreds of responses we gathered, I became even more aware that charisma meant different things to different people and that I needed to create my own definition. Charismatic leadership will be effective, both in the short and long term. Uncharismatic leadership will be most effective in the short term (as anybody who has ever needed to get a teenage son or daughter out of the house to a tight deadline will testify), but it won't captivate hearts and minds. Each and every one of us has the potential to be both charismatic and uncharismatic. This shared inconsistency in others makes charisma even harder to define. So what is it not? Charisma is not confidence; you don't need to have a big maverick personality to possess it. You don't need to shout or show off. Charisma is not charm and it does not appear when you develop other communication skills.

Learning from charismatic icons

I studied the behaviours of four charismatic icons who had been filmed in many different situations: Margaret Thatcher, Martin Luther King, Muhammad Ali and Elvis Presley. These individuals, in my view, exhibited extremely high levels of charisma. Yet it was a challenge to find behavioural similarities. Margaret Thatcher used eye contact as a decisive, authoritative tool, whilst many of Elvis Presley's most memorable performances were sung with his eyes closed. Martin Luther King spoke of peace with inflamed vocal oratory. Muhammad Ali, who as a boxer made his name in an aggressive sport, spoke quickly with wit, humour and fast animated hand gestures. Thatcher and Ali both raved about their successes, regularly playing to the crowd, whilst King's oratories appeared ignited with religious fervour and powerful metaphors. I noticed that Presley often appeared humble and awkward when he wasn't 'performing', especially during interviews when he stumbled over his choice of words. This gave me my first clue to the theory that charisma is contextual. Someone might be extremely charismatic in one context yet possess no charisma in another. My initial theory that any individual can become charismatic simply by replicating specific charismatic behaviours was completely wrong. As these charismatic icons demonstrate, they each show their charisma using different types of behaviours. Charismatic people stand out not because of their behaviours, but because of something innate within them that commands and compels our attention.

An inside-out approach

Inspired by Louise Hay (2004), renowned author and lecturer on the impact of thoughts on the body ('when we really love ourselves, everything in our life works'), I began exploring whether charisma can be developed by adopting an 'inside-out' approach. In other words, the external behaviours exhibited by charismatic people are a 'reaction to' or an 'effect of' an internal cause. I started looking at the inside causes of external charismatic effects. For example, charismatic people are passionate about what they do, yet each charismatic person manifests their passion in their own unique way. Martin Luther King's body language, including his facial expressions, were relatively low key during his famous 'I have a Dream' speech. His biblical cadences, the evocative pictures he painted and his evangelical delivery were behavioural expressions of the passion he felt. Contrast these behaviours with those that Muhammad Ali demonstrated before a big fight when speaking of his desire to win. Ali would talk quickly with high energy and paint pictures with his hands. His vocal range was varied and sprinkled with lots of commanding tonality. Both Martin Luther King and Muhammad Ali were passionate about their lives yet each man expressed their passion with different behaviours. Imagine if Muhammad Ali tried to emulate Martin Luther King's behaviours. He would have appeared fake and lacking in authenticity. Charismatic people speak with their heart and soul. If you try to emulate Martin Luther King or any other charismatic individual you admire, you are effectively putting on a mask that causes you to emulate behaviours that are not necessarily a reflection of the real authentic you. This immediately dilutes your emotional intensity and inhibits the flow of your natural charisma. If you are not behaving in alignment with who you truly are, then others will unconsciously and often consciously sense that something just isn't right about you, and they will disconnect from you emotionally.

Behavioural Similarities Chart

This chart shows the frequency of different behaviours demonstrated by King, Presley, Thatcher and Ali in video footage extracts viewed on YouTube. By summarising this information in a chart format you can see that there is no clear trend of specific charismatic behaviours that are always demonstrated by every charismatic individual.

– Behavioural similarities chart –

Behaviours	Martin Luther King	Elvis Presley	Magaret Thatcher	Muhammad Ali
Eye contact	2	1	3	3
Animated facial expression	1	2	3	3
Use of strong hand gestures	1	2	3	3
Natural smile	2	1	1	3
Varied voice tone and pace	3	1	2	2
Fast talking pace	1	1	2	3
Commanding voice tonality	2	1	3	2
Use of pauses	2	1	1	3
Centred body posture	3	2	3	3
Clear diction	3	1	3	1
Actively listens	2	1	2	1
Large vocabulary	3	1	3	2
Adaptable	2	1	2	2
High physical energy	3	3	3	3
Appears enthusiastic	3	3	3	3
Open body language	2	1	3	3
Resonant voice	3	2	3	2
Appears confident	3	2	3	3
Expert on their subject	3	3	3	3
Uses stories and metaphors	3	1	2	3
Shows conviction	3	3	3	3

Key (number of apples): Sometimes demonstrated (1) · Regularly demonstrated (2) · Frequently demonstrated (3)

Published in 2008 – Releasing Your Hidden Charisma by Nikki Owen and updated in 2013.

My definition of charisma

I define charisma as an authentic power that captivates the hearts and minds of others. To put it another way, when you are being you and you love what you do – you shine. This definition begins to explain why charisma is contextual. The charismatic individual who shines in a career context can be almost invisible in a social or home environment. A performer or a politician may dazzle when they are in the public eye, because what they are doing is important to them. Put them in another setting and they merge to become one of the crowd. If the late Martin Luther King was asked to deliver a speech on boxing, would his passion, authenticity and charisma have shone through in the same way? This definition differs from the stereotypical view in two key ways. I do not believe that an extrovert or having a 'big personality' is a prerequisite to being charismatic. On the contrary, the single most important factor that determines an individual's charisma is the extent that they are able to 'captivate hearts and minds'. Often you'll find that quietly confident, introverted people are every bit as charismatic as their more self-publicising counterparts.

Charisma and introverts

This view is supported by a study published in the December 2010 issue of the Harvard Business Review (Grant et al., 2010) showing that the more reserved style of introverted leaders can actually inspire better performance in followers. Researchers Adam Grant of the Wharton School, Francesca Gino of Harvard Business School and David Hofmann at the University of North Carolina found that if the employees are an extroverted, proactive bunch by nature, the team will perform better under the leadership of an introvert than under an extrovert. The study goes on to explain that introverted leaders are more likely to take a team approach to problem solving and to let talented team members spread their wings. Within my own experience I am sure that we can all think back to leaders, managers, teachers or mentors who have patiently drawn out our opinions, encouraged our creativity and have genuinely valued and shown appreciation for our contributions to the achievement of a collective goal. These people may not all have met the regulation blueprint of a charismatic leader, but they managed to 'captivate our hearts and minds' nonetheless. When we think of charismatic and introverted people who have had enormous impact on the world, there are many examples. Mahatma Ghandi, Meryl Streep, Steve Jobs, Albert Einstein, Princess Diana and even Robbie Williams often showed a quiet vulnerability that somewhat disproves the claim that you need to be an extrovert to be charismatic.

Charisma and authenticity

The key to charisma is authenticity. One of the most exciting television projects I did was as an official political commentator for Aljazeera during the 2010 live UK election debates. This project stands out because it was the first time that political leaders engaged in a live televised debate. Working with the Professor of British Politics (who was required to commentate on the leaders' policies), my role was to commentate on their authenticity and charisma. I remember watching Gordon Brown as his insecurities around being pitted against his two younger adversaries were demonstrated in the form of aggressive and often rude behaviour. Shortly afterwards I watched Gordon give his resignation speech that he had written himself (Brown, 2010). As he spoke from his heart, his warmth and 'humanness' shone through and I wondered why he had not just been himself during the live political debates. In business, as in politics, alarm bells start to ring when a leader's 'from the heart' emotional response seems a bit too coached. I remember watching Tony Blair in 1997 as he announced the death of Princess Diana. I was filled with a sense that he was delivering a brilliant speech designed to tug at our heart strings. It felt a bit too contrived. When the words just don't match the body language, and especially when our hardwired unconscious mind feels that there is something less than authentic about them, we will experience a negative reaction that we often can't quite explain logically. This may well be why we love our sporting heroes to be charismatic in the absolute stereotypical – big, brash, confident – sense of the word. When Muhammad Ali, with absolute unshakeable self-confidence, stared down the camera and stated that he was 'The Greatest', we believed him, and we didn't start looking for any hidden agendas, because there were none. I would go as far as to say that we expect our sporting heroes' self-esteem to be developed close to the point of arrogance, otherwise it just doesn't seem authentic. Unconsciously we question whether they have that all-important 'will to win'. Andy

Murray won more fans for losing to Federer at Wimbledon in 2012, and letting us see just how much that loss hurt him, than he did by reversing the result several weeks later at the Olympics. Conversely, because we have a fundamental belief that politicians are – first and foremost – public servants, for us to see them as authentic (and therefore charismatic), we need them to show far more humility than our ego driven sporting heroes. Our political leaders draw their charismatic appeal not from their displays of confidence or self-esteem, but from their vision, driving force and devotion to their mission or purpose. People believed in Nelson Mandela because he showed that, with his suffering and sacrifice, he really cared. Nobody could ever doubt that Gandhi wasn't passionate about the plight of his people, or that Martin Luther King had a dream that became more real than his harsh reality.

Authenticity creates an emotional connection

In business, the leaders that we recognise as being truly charismatic have the ability to walk that fine line between letting us see that they possess huge drive to be successful, whilst at the same time demonstrating an appreciation and understanding of their ethical and social responsibilities. The really interesting thing is that, in business, as in politics and sport, at the point when a charismatic leader ceases to be authentic, at the moment when he or she fails to connect at an emotional level, their charisma is lost, and the spell is broken. If an individual lacks authenticity, if they don't mean what they say, they dilute the strength of their character and consequently the strength of their charisma. Some individuals compensate for their lack of internal and external congruency by over-developing their external charm. If you try to emulate any other charismatic individual you are effectively acting and wearing a mask of charisma. Whatever external mask you choose to wear, if it doesn't reflect the genuine, authentic 'you' this will automatically convey a superficial aspect to your personality. The only way to be truly charismatic is to be authentic and to speak from your heart.

Heartfelt communication

In our western culture, many of the leaders that I have worked with feel uncomfortable when they see that part of my charisma definition mentions *heart.* Many organisations already have strong and robust processes in place to build employee engagement. Leadership teams are generally good at winning the *minds* of their people. Engagement and motivation are emotional responses, an unconscious as well as a conscious desire to work with heart and soul for the benefit of their leader and their organisation. When leaders cannot communicate with their heart, and find it difficult to express their emotional side, they generally struggle to build engagement, and often encounter even more resistance to changed ways of working. Heartfelt communication triggers serotonin and oxytocin – hormones that naturally increases empathy, positivity and trust.

Charisma and the vagus nerve

There is a scientific explanation that explains why some leaders can evoke a strong positive emotional response and attract massive followership. The vagus nerve is a bundle of nerves that originates in the top of the spinal cord. It activates different organs throughout the body (such as the heart, lungs, liver and digestive organs). When active, it is likely to produce that feeling of warm expansion in the chest – for example when we are moved by someone's goodness or when we appreciate a beautiful piece of music. Neuroscientist Stephen W. Porges of the University of Illinois in Chicago (2010) refers to the vagus nerve as the nerve of compassion. This is because it stimulates certain muscles in the vocal chamber, enabling communication to flow, and it reduces the heart rate to promote a feeling of calm. Studies suggest that there is a connection with oxytocin, a neurotransmitter involved in trust and empathy. Consequently, the vagus nerve is associated with feelings of caretaking and the ethical intuition that humans from different social groups (even adversarial ones) share a common humanity. People who have high vagus nerve activation in a resting state are more likely to be altruistic, compassionate, feel gratitude, love and happiness. A person with genuine charisma boosts the vagus nerve activators and draws people towards them effortlessly in an almost unconscious manner.

Born with charisma

In a sense I agree with experts who say that *charisma cannot be taught* because charisma is an attribute that is already within us. You don't have to become someone different to become more charismatic. When you reconnect with who you really are inside you'll instantly light up your energy and your presence. Think about the attention a tiny baby creates. As we grow up, we learn how to play different roles that make it harder for us to remember the charisma we have inside. We wear different 'faces' to mask how we really feel. 'I'm fine' is the biggest lie that millions of people tell every day. I once read a report about a high powered city business woman who has extensive Botox specifically so she can look neutral in meetings, fearing that her emotions may betray what she really feels inside. This struck me as intensely sad. In some corporate arenas, it's not politically correct to show any emotion; in fact, some business people see emotion as a sign of weakness. Emotions play a far greater role in determining business outcomes across industries than many executives grasp, as Gallup research continues to demonstrate. Classical economic theory states that people make decisions by processing a set of objective information based on a rational economic model. Yet senior scientists in the field of behavioural economics acknowledge that human beings are *not entirely rational in their decision making*. Those organisations who understand the role emotions play in predicting outcomes will ultimately perform better. Charismatic leaders emotionally engage their employees because they are comfortable with engaging their own emotional responses.

Charisma evokes an emotional reaction

This is more than just an abstract theory as scientists have now proved that our heart really does rule our head. According to research, the part of the brain used for cold, hard analysis is suppressed when we hear a sad story. US scientists scanned the brains of 45 young men and women as they solved problems, half of which required them to think about how others feel, whilst the other questions were based on physics. The scans revealed that while the participants were thinking about other people, the empathy network of the brain fired up, overriding the analytical part. The reverse occurred while they were thinking about physics. It is difficult to empathise and analyse at the same time. Charismatic leaders lead with their hearts, not just their minds. They are not afraid to show their emotions and seek to connect with their employees and followers. This does not mean charismatic leaders are *soft*, it simply means that they are prepared to 'be themselves' rather than wear a mask or play a particular role.

Charisma with compassion

Charisma is a power. It has the power to motivate millions to create massive engagement and followship. Charisma has a powerful impact on others. Do you remember the advice given to Peter Parker (Spiderman) by his Uncle Ben, 'With great power comes great responsibility'? History has shown the damage that charismatic leaders with evil intent towards others can wield. Quantum physics shows that at a subatomic level we are all interconnected energetically. Our thoughts, feelings and actions affect those around us. When we continue to persevere with the old myth that we are separate from everyone or everything on the planet, it becomes easier to judge and harm others. According to Albert Einstein (Calaprice, 2005),

> A human being is part of the whole that we call the universe. He experiences himself, his thoughts and feelings, as something separated from the rest – a kind of optical illusion of his consciousness. Our task must be to free ourselves from this prison by widening our circle of compassion to embrace all living things and all of nature.

This level of compassion is vital when developing charisma because it ensures the ecology of the leader's message on all living things. Mahatma Gandhi, Jesus Christ and Cheng Yen, the Taiwanese Buddhist nun who leads a worldwide social welfare movement, are examples of this blend of compassionate charisma.

Remembering who we truly are

When it comes down to increasing your charisma you don't need to learn anything new. You simply have to feel comfortable being you, connect with your emotions and find purpose and personal meaning in your everyday work. This may sound simplistic yet it takes real courage to remain fundamentally true to who we really are inside – with every individual we meet – and in every context. Years of environmental conditioning often stops us from allowing our softer and, therefore, more vulnerable side to show. Once we start to honour our true self we experience a feeling of euphoria at the sheer sensation of being alive.

Chapter 2

The reality we create

To fully appreciate how to enhance your charisma, it helps to understand the process that occurs as we communicate. When you are feeling truly happy you are in a peak performing state. This state is described by Hungarian psychologist Mihaly Csikszentmihalyi as a state of flow. This is when you are so immersed in what you are doing that all your attention and motivation energises and absorbs you to the extent that everything appears effortless and time appears suspended. Mihaly estimated that every moment our unconscious mind absorbs around 2 million bits of information through our senses. Professor of Psychology George Miller at Harvard University (1956) suggests that our conscious minds can only process around seven chunks of information at any given moment. Take a moment and try and recall as many different car manufacturers you can think of within 30 seconds. Notice where you pause. Often it will be after recalling five, six or seven manufacturers' names. This signals that your conscious mind is 'full' and needs to clear this information so that you can access additional information stored within your unconscious mind. This means that you can never, consciously, really know reality or what's really going on 'out there' – the only reality that makes sense is the one that you create inside your mind. Consequently, everyone's perception of reality is different and everyone's internal reality is true for them.

Your goldmine

Imagine that there are two buckets in front of you: one contains all the information from your unconscious mind and the other contains all the information from your conscious mind. As you notice the vast difference in the quantity of information contained within the two buckets, think about all that untapped wisdom you actually possess. You have access to a goldmine of resources that you can explore and discover whenever you want. In a business context most western people and organisations are conditioned to rely more on their conscious mind, facts, statistics and processes rather than to listen to the whispers of insight from their unconscious mind. 'Gut feel' and intuition have been replaced by the logical reasoning of the much more limited conscious mind. The unconscious mind holds so much more information compared to the conscious mind. Sir Francis Bacon, in 1597, first referred to knowledge as a power and implied that gaining and sharing knowledge increases an individual's potential and their abilities in life. So why aren't contemporary business leaders actively encouraging employees to trust their instincts and listen to the wise whispers of knowledge that stream from the unconscious mind? The beliefs and values from your unconscious mind are not restricted by any filters processed by your conscious mind and the prime directive from your unconscious mind is to protect you and keep you safe.

– CHARISMA ENHANCER –

Tune into and act upon your intuition. Its roots are located within your unconscious mind. This rich goldmine of information communicates with your conscious mind using insights and emotions. When you are really tuned into someone to a level where you feel that connection, you begin to access your intuition. This process gives you the ability to know something directly without analytic reasoning and you bridge the gap between the conscious and unconscious parts of your mind. Working in partnership with your intuition will deepen your level of communication enabling the other person to express their true feelings with greater ease. We can't control the outside world regardless of what's going on around us, yet we can accept guidance from our wise intuitive unconscious mind.

Delete and distort

You don't need to be a maths genius to recognise that most of the information that enters our unconscious mind is deleted when it filters into our conscious mind. We also distort information as it filters into our conscious awareness. How often have you said something to someone with a really good intention but the other person completely misunderstood the intention behind what you were trying to communicate? This happens even more frequently with emails and texts. When you erase the voice tonality component and the look on someone's face, then the meaning behind bare words is interpreted in a variety of different ways. Have you ever noticed that your thinking gets distorted when you are feeling stressed? Decisions that you make under pressure may not be the decisions you would have chosen to make if you had been feeling calm and relaxed. I remember an incident when I was 12. My parents had gone out for a few hours to

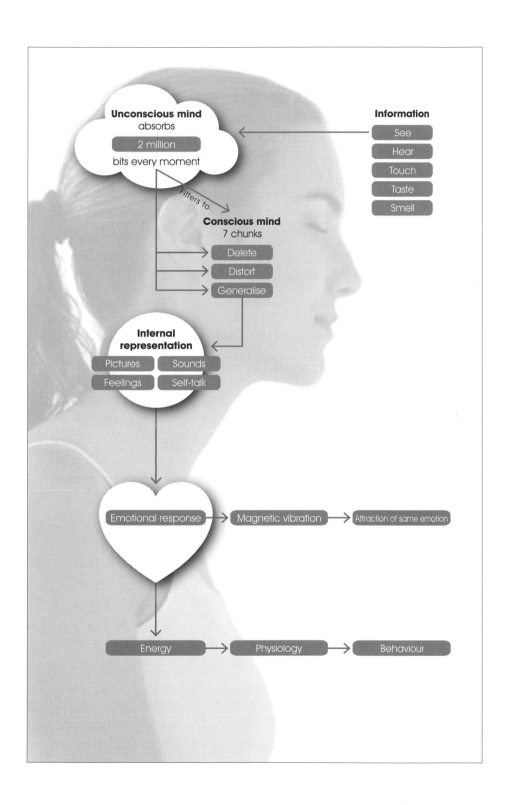

have drinks with our neighbours. It was the first time I had been left to look after my younger sister and brother. After getting them into bed I waited for my parents to come home. I was suddenly aware of someone creeping around the house. I was so scared that I felt frozen with fear. As this 'person' began to walk up the stairs I realised that it wasn't an intruder or a burglar. I was distorting the sounds of the central heating system, the same sounds that I heard every night. Because my parents were not home and I felt anxious, I had distorted these familiar sounds into the sound of a burglar! My body's physiological reaction could not tell the difference between what was real and what was imagined. My mouth went dry, my heart was racing, responding to the fear I was feeling, even though this 'burglar' was just a figment of my vivid imagination.

Generalisations

During the first six years of our life we operate in a hypnogogic state when our unconscious mind dominates our conscious mind, which is why young children learn and absorb so much during this period. As we grow older our conscious mind tends to take over and we make generalisations of our experiences. When we see a chair that we have never seen before, our conscious mind categorises it into 'chair'. We expect to pull door handles downwards to open them. These are just some examples of generalisations that help our conscious mind to process all the information that it can potentially process. Our beliefs can often be generalisations that were determined when we were very young. When my former partner was about three years old he tried to climb up onto the top of his mum's cooker and pulled a saucepan of boiling milk onto himself. Using techniques that helped him to revisit that memory, he recalls making the decision when he was a toddler, 'It's not safe to climb too high.' As an adult he often sabotaged his career when it looked as if he was about to be promoted. The generalisation he formed at three years old continued to create an unconscious impact on him for 50 years until he was able to resolve it.

Inside our head

Once information has been filtered into our conscious awareness, four things happen. We create pictures, hear sounds, feel physiological feelings and we talk to ourselves. How we portray these internal representations affects our emotional reaction. For example, create a picture of someone you love inside your mind. Does the intensity of your love change if you make the picture larger? By changing the way we represent information internally we then have the opportunity to create a change in our emotional response. We can't change the past, yet we can change our emotional reaction to the past. Imagine two women waiting in a restaurant for their partners who are late showing up. The first woman sees a picture of her partner in a car crash, hears imaginary sirens inside her head and repeats to herself, 'Oh no, what if he's had an accident?' The second woman sees a picture of her partner flirting with his new attractive marketing executive. This woman keeps saying to herself, 'Can I trust him anymore?' Now play out the scene and imagine both men entering the restaurant. The first woman runs up to her partner and hugs him saying, 'Thank goodness you are OK', whilst the second woman stomps out of the restaurant in a huff! Both women were in the same situation, yet their internal processing created two very different emotional responses. The issue facing an individual is not really about the issue, it's about the individual's emotional reaction to their issue. If the negative emotions attached to their issue are released, then their issue becomes a non-issue. The majority of work-related issues that dominate my one-to-one sessions with clients are focused around toxic relationships with peers, colleagues or bosses. Initially, people believe that they have no relationship or link with the 'other person' and might adopt the view that it's futile to fret over the relationship because they have no control over the other person's behaviour. This is when it gets interesting. If you accept the difference in the amount of information that flows into your conscious and unconscious mind, then your reality is based on your perception of reality. The illusion of a toxic relationship only exists inside you. To put it another way, if you resolve the toxic relationship inside your head, you clear up the toxic relationship within your external reality.

Changing your emotional responses

In the early 1990s my autobiography, *Nicola – A Second Chance to Live* (1992), was published in both hardback and paperback in 16 countries. The publishers, Transworld Publishing, wanted me to participate in an extensive publicity itinerary to promote sales of my book. I was scheduled to appear on a British chat show presented by Richard Madeley and Judy

Finnigan. The television studio had arranged a courtesy car to collect me. I was told there would be a male guest in the car. Hoping it would be Brad Pitt I was slightly mollified when in the back seat I recognised Paul McKenna, presenter of *The Hypnotic World of Paul McKenna*. He was wearing a royal blue jacket and a warm smile. We chatted for 30 minutes about my work on charisma and his new television show when he said casually, 'Nikki, do you realise that you can change how you feel in an instant?' I reacted with caustic scepticism. Did he know what a difficult past I had and how I still had strong emotional flashbacks? Paul's sensory awareness was really sharp and without skipping a beat he asked me to think about someone in my life who really frustrated me. I instantly thought of this intensely irritating 'acquaintance' who was incredibly 'hyper'. I felt exhausted every time we met. She talked really quickly, often invaded my personal space by shoving her face really close to mine and showered me with saliva… aagh! Paul immediately asked me to imagine her as so tiny that I could see her standing on my knee. He then asked me to visualise her jumping up and down and chattering in a cartoon voice – 'Nikki! Notice Me!' I fell about laughing. Paul had just proved that in a few seconds I had changed my emotional reaction towards her from intense irritation to one of relaxed amusement.

– CHARISMA ENHANCER –

Think about someone who irritates or annoys you. Notice the size of the picture you have of them in your mind's eye. What happens to your feelings if you make that picture smaller? What are you saying to yourself? What if you changed your voice tone so it was soothing and comforting? What if you imagined picking up this person and placing them onto your desk? What if you had a magic remote control and could press 'pause' on their ability to move at any point? These questions are to show you how you can change your emotional responses by changing the way you represent this person in your mind.

Point of power

So many times, our internal representations can induce negative or unhelpful emotional reactions and we think there is nothing we can do about it. Yet we can. This knowledge is key to our ability to access our point of real power. If you are about to deliver a presentation and in your mind you see the audience looking bored or intimidating, then it's likely you'll feel anxiety and fear. If you imagine the audience smiling and clapping, then this instantly changes your emotional reaction. I remember a time in my life when I used to feel petrified about picking up the phone and making a business call. This 'call reluctance' was a real issue until my boss and dynamic mentor suggested that I imagine that the person I was calling was sitting on a toilet. I laughed, felt more relaxed and found picking up the phone easy because of this unusual vision in my head!

Emotional frequencies

Our emotional reaction determines the frequency that we transmit and receive information on. When we tune into a particular radio station we are tuning into a particular frequency that enables us to connect with that specific radio programme. Human beings are like satellites – our body is an antenna, designed to pick up thousands of signals from our environment. Every emotion has a vibrational frequency that informs your reticular activating system (RAS), which is a set of nuclei connected in the brain. This RAS exercises great influence over our cognitive capabilities and categorises our experiences based on what it perceives as 'important' from 'unimportant'. Our thoughts determine our emotional response and our emotions are the criteria by which RAS makes its categorisation. If we are feeling angry then we activate our angry frequency and connect with information in our environment that notices and validates anger. This is why we appear to attract what we are feeling. Have you ever wondered why some people sail through life attracting opportunities, good fortune and wonderful experiences whilst others appear to struggle from hardship to hardship? People who are transmitting on a frequency of anger can only really connect with anger on this frequency. Anything on a different emotional frequency cannot be accessed. You can't tune into one radio station and hear another radio station, can you? Universal law states that everything in the universe moves and vibrates at one speed or another. Everything you see around you is vibrating at one frequency or another, as are you. When your frequency is markedly different from another person's frequency you'll feel separate and isolated from them.

We are energy beings

Quantum physics deals with the behaviour of the smallest things in our universe – subatomic particles. Scientists at the frontiers of research in this field have demonstrated that each particle is made out of smaller subatomic particles that are not made of matter. They are packets of pulsating energy that constantly interact with our environment. What we thought was physical is not physical. At its smallest, everything in this universe is made out of immaterial energy, and everything radiates energy. The chair that you're sitting on is comprised of energy. This book is energy. The walls of the room that you are now in, your computer, the events that happen to you are all made up of vibrations of energy. And your thoughts, too, are vibrations of energy. Your thoughts are of the exact same substance as the building blocks of the universe because everything is based on vibration. Once we become aware of this remarkable fact, we can use it to our great advantage. Every molecule and atom radiates and absorbs light (energy) and because we are made out of these atoms and molecules we are constantly radiating energy as a vibration. This vibrating energy will appear more or less dense based on its vibrational frequency. To understand why we can appear to be solid, take water as an example. When it's cold it freezes and becomes ice. When it's hot it becomes steam. The vibrational frequencies for ice and steam vary. Your energies are constantly moving, interacting and affecting other energies within your environment. At an energetic level, every thought you have affects everything. Modern physics now sees the universe as a vast, inseparable web of dynamic activity. Not only is the universe alive and constantly changing, but everything in the universe affects everything else. At its most primary level, the universe seems to be whole and undifferentiated, a fathomless sea of energy that permeates every object and every act. It is all one. In short, scientists are now confirming what mystics and seers have been telling us for thousands of years – we are not separate from but part of one whole.

The law of attraction

The law of attraction is the name given to the belief that 'like attracts like' or things with similar vibrational frequencies are attracted to each other. By focusing on either positive or negative thoughts, and understanding

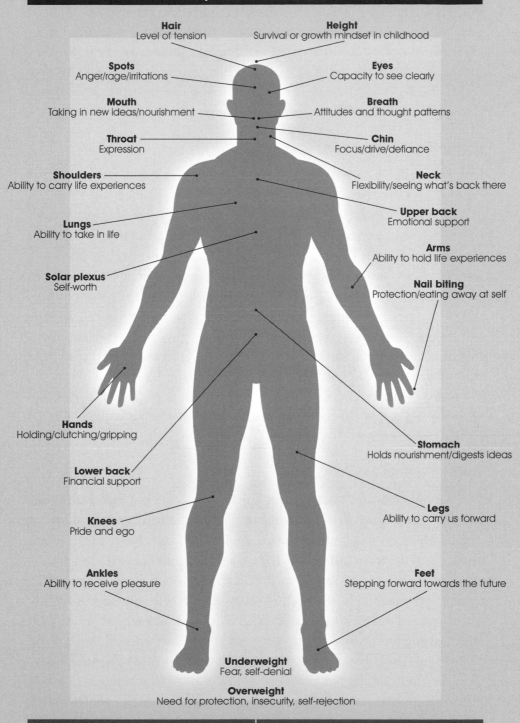

– Physical indicators –

Hair
Level of tension

Height
Survival or growth mindset in childhood

Spots
Anger/rage/irritations

Eyes
Capacity to see clearly

Mouth
Taking in new ideas/nourishment

Breath
Attitudes and thought patterns

Throat
Expression

Chin
Focus/drive/defiance

Shoulders
Ability to carry life experiences

Neck
Flexibility/seeing what's back there

Upper back
Emotional support

Lungs
Ability to take in life

Arms
Ability to hold life experiences

Solar plexus
Self-worth

Nail biting
Protection/eating away at self

Hands
Holding/clutching/gripping

Stomach
Holds nourishment/digests ideas

Lower back
Financial support

Knees
Pride and ego

Legs
Ability to carry us forward

Ankles
Ability to receive pleasure

Feet
Stepping forward towards the future

Underweight
Fear, self-denial

Overweight
Need for protection, insecurity, self-rejection

Female energy – mother

Male energy – father

that each type has different vibrational frequencies, you can bring about positive or negative results. Everything is connected by a vast quantum energy field and can be influenced by thought. These laws from quantum mechanics also point to strong evidence that the observer has an effect on reality. Every thought creates an energetic impulse and there is evidence that our thoughts have the capacity to change physical matter.

Physiological response

Every thought we have triggers an emotional response that impacts on our physiology. Conversely, the way we move our body will affect our emotions and thoughts. Thoughts, emotions and physiology are interconnected. Changing one or more of the trio impacts on the other two. If a person thinks they are not good enough (thought), they may feel embarrassed (emotional response) and they blush (impact on physiology). According to 1981 Nobel Prize winner Roger W. Sperry each side of the brain controls different types of thinking. The left brain tends to favour logical, analytical, objective and process thinking while the right brain tends to favour intuitive, creative and subjective thinking. The left brain operates the right side of the body and the right brain operates the left side of the body. Typically, the left brain is associated with male energy and the right brain with female energy. Therefore you can identify whether an individual is led by their heart or by their head based on their physicality.

Your body does not lie

During my charisma masterclasses I give attendees feedback within ten minutes of meeting them based on my observations of their physiology. The depth of my observations creates shock that I am able to see so much about them in such a short time. Everyone has the ability to do this by understanding how emotional issues are held in the body. Look at yourself in a full length mirror. Notice whether your shoulders are balanced. A slightly raised right shoulder may indicate that you have unresolved issues with your father from when you were younger. (People who flinch tend to raise their shoulder.) Is your chin and neck jutting out in front of your body? This may indicate that you are very driven and quick thinking. That you lead with your head rather than with your emotions and can get frustrated that others can't keep up with you – even your body can't keep pace with your speed of thought. If you have tightness across your shoulders this may be because you are feeling the weight of your responsibilities or are carrying a burden. Do you pull back slightly from your upper ribcage area – causing your head to move downwards? This may be a sign that you have low self-esteem and don't feel good enough. When you speak do you breathe from your throat? This usually indicates that you struggle to express how you really feel about things. Do you have spots, blemishes or acne? Who are you feeling irritated with? What's making you angry and getting under your skin? Your body contains so much valuable feedback around whether or not you are living your life in balance. When your thoughts are positive, supportive and empowering you experience emotional balance and your body reflects this internal alignment. Any physical imbalance may well be your unconscious mind trying to gain your attention towards something that is starting to affect your health and well-being. I remember hearing the expression, 'You get the face you deserve.' This is so true. Look at people who are embittered by the cruel challenges life has inflicted upon them – pain is etched into their face and body. Your body is a powerful indicator of what you have been feeling over a period of time. Chronic stress from negative attitudes and feelings of helplessness and hopelessness can upset the body's hormone balance. This depletes the brain's messenger chemicals required for feeling happiness and has a damaging impact on the immune system. New scientific understandings have identified the process by which chronic stress can actually decrease our lifespan by shortening our telomeres (the 'end caps' of our DNA strands, which play a big role in ageing). Poorly managed or repressed anger (hostility) is also related to a slew of health conditions, such as hypertension, cardiovascular disease, digestive disorders and infection. Your body does not lie.

Behaviour

If thoughts affect our emotions that manifest in our body, then it follows that our behaviour is affected also by our thoughts. If we are feeling powerful, we energise and strengthen our physiology and this will impact upon our behaviour. Just think about how you behave when you are feeling a) nervous and b) confident. Many organisations wanting to improve or change the behaviours of their workforce struggle to do this because they believe that by telling or showing someone how to behave is sufficient to ensure behavioural change. Because so much of our negative programming is often unconscious, our behaviour is often unconscious and change becomes incredibly difficult. Simply by changing the way we think, we change our emotional response, which affects our vibrational frequency and delivers a different behavioural output. Rather than seek to change your behaviour by working on the same logical level of behaviour, seek to change and sustain behaviour by first changing your thinking. Teaching 'charismatic behaviours' will not create a charismatic person for two main reasons: each person's underlying thoughts have an impact on their behaviour and each person's charisma will be expressed differently. The first step to increasing your charisma is to adopt an inside-out approach by taking back control of your thoughts. Would you prefer driving your own bus or being a passenger on a bus? When you begin to have thoughts aligned to your core self then your behaviours become an authentic expression of who you really are inside. Mindfulness is the practice of purposely focusing your attention on the present moment and accepting it without judgement. By becoming more mindful of the thoughts that are flowing in and out of your awareness you are starting to exercise more control over the way you live your life. Charisma starts with a thought, an intention that starts a sequence of events that will be manifested in your own behaviour. So if you're serious about developing your charisma then start meditating to still the monkey chatter in your mind.

– CHARISMA ENHANCER –

One of my favourite ways to take back control of your thoughts is to bring your negative thoughts to the attention of your conscious mind. As you start to notice these types of thoughts you can start to 'interrupt' your ability to think negatively. Find an elastic band that fits comfortably around your wrist – tight enough to be noticeable, but without restricting your blood flow. Every time you notice you are having a negative thought, switch the rubber band to your other wrist. If you do this for three or four days you'll be amazed at the speed with which you can reduce your negative thoughts.

Chapter 3

The blueprint for charisma

E very individual's perception of their environment is subjective. Their perception is true for that individual. Personal transformation can be achieved simply by shifting and expanding this perspective. Many people look outside to gain knowledge that enables them to widen their perceptions and understanding. Yet you have an extraordinary level of inner wisdom, direct knowing and subjective understanding that you can leverage to increase your knowledge of how to access the expanded state of charisma. By drawing upon scientific principles, psychology and extensive research-based studies and combining these with esoteric philosophies, I created my own internal blueprint for charisma. Authentic charisma is built upon the degree to which five internal attributes, referred to as pillars, have been developed:

1. Self-esteem
2. Sensory awareness
3. Compelling vision
4. Driving force
5. Balanced energy

Each pillar has been built based on the beliefs, values and experiences of your past programming. If your parents wanted you to do well at school and kept pushing you to get better examination results, then you may have unwittingly felt that anything less than 100 per cent was not good enough. As a child this might have contributed towards a deeply held belief that you are not good enough generally. This type of belief erodes self-esteem. Imagine being raised in an environment where money was scarce and feeling a strong parental fear of lack of money. This may have accelerated a strong driving force to be successful and create high levels of wealth. Irrespective of whether your past programming was good or bad it has shaped the individual you are today. The construction and constituents of each pillar is expressed through a variety of unconscious behaviours that in a work context influences a leader's impact (either positively or negatively). If the programming from your childhood has created an imbalance within one or more of the pillars, this will reduce your personal magnetism and charisma. A deficit in these pillars will be manifested in a leader in a number of negative attitudes and behaviours that will have an impact within the organisation.

− Self-esteem −			
High levels	Leadership impact	Low levels	Leadership impact
Comfortable, grounded	Creates a safe environment	Defensive, hypersensitive	Creates an environment of fear
Authentic, genuine	Builds collaboration	Boastful, arrogant	Builds silos
Inner confidence	Develops others' confidence	Craves constant feedback	Competitive versus collaborative culture
Open, at ease with self	Increases trust and builds self-worth	Self-critical, perfectionism	Drains others' confidence

− Sensory awareness −			
High levels	Leadership impact	Low levels	Leadership impact
Compassionate, caring	Encourages 'from the heart' communication	Contained, reserved	Struggles with engagement
Emotionally intelligent	Deepens the quality of working relationships	Inconsiderate, lacks empathy	Aloof and unapproachable
Evokes emotions	Increases engagement, motivation and followship	Distant, aloof, unaware	Alienates creative and amiable types
Strong trust, relationships	Improves connections and a collaborative approach	Judgemental, cold	Lacks perception and intuition

− Compelling vision −			
High levels	Leadership impact	Low levels	Leadership impact
Inspirational, stimulating	Increases creativity and growth	Overly detailed, logical	Activates disengagement
Captivating, thought-provoking	Supports in-depth reflection	Indecisive, 'grey', aimless	Uninspiring
Exciting, visionary	Increased alignment with corporate vision	Lacks purpose, personal meaning	Creates apathy, resistance and demotivation
Pioneering, innovative	Stimulates courage and change agent	Procrastination, stagnation	Comfort zone performance

– Driving force –			
High levels	Leadership impact	Low levels	Leadership impact
Enthusiastic, dynamic	Builds energy within the workplace	Ineffectual, indecisive	Disengaged and disengages
Passionate, motivational	Creates peak performance	Apathetic, fearful	Distracted and low output
Achiever, optimistic	Role model of excellence	Unproductive, inefficient	Drains energy and stifles innovation
Courageous, resilient	Inspires 'out of the box' thinking	Negative, pessimistic	Creates inefficiency

– Balanced energy –			
High levels	Leadership impact	Low levels	Leadership impact
Stimulating, exciting	Inspires innovation and peak performance	Low energy, complainer	Creates stress and fear
Fit, healthy, balanced	Ensures employees are 'in flow'	Low resilience, poor health	More prone to illness
Powerful, influential	Boosts energy and engagement	Victim, poor me	Over-emotional
Achiever, change agent	Role model of excellence – proof that 'it can be done'	Wired, snappy, unpredictable	Negative, isolated, silos

Supporting your charismatic growth

Everything has a vibrational frequency. Therefore as you start to open up yourself to allowing your own charisma to grow and flourish you'll need to begin operating within a vibrational frequency that supports this growth. Identifying the pillar or pillars where your levels are low provides you with a place to start when developing your own charisma. Be honest with yourself and accept 100 per cent responsibility for who you are and what you are creating in all aspects of your life. This ensures that your mindset is in a state of readiness to transcend from where you are now to where you want to be.

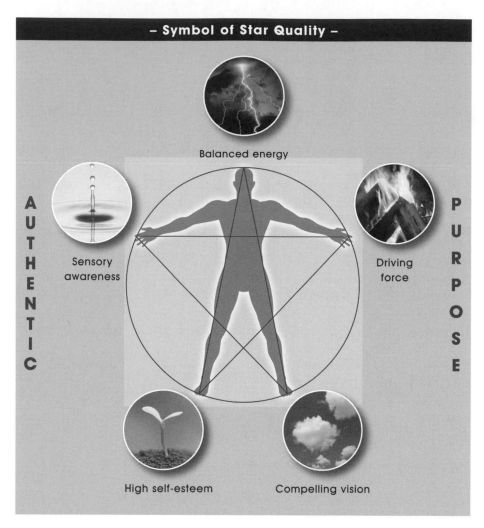

- Symbol of Star Quality -

Balanced energy

AUTHENTIC

Sensory awareness

PURPOSE

Driving force

High self-esteem

Compelling vision

Symbology and metaphor to promote understanding

Swiss psychiatrist and analyst Carl Gustav Jung used symbols as an easy way to identify different personality archetypes. Throughout history, symbols have possessed a power that can unite different themes, such as the symbol in Chinese philosophy, yin yang, that blends two polarities of masculine and feminine energy. The characteristics of the five pillars of charisma are better understood when they are related, symbolised and metaphorically linked to the universal laws of nature. As I began working on how to best present the five pillars of charisma I noticed that each pillar shared characteristics with the elements of nature.

Is your self-esteem down-to-earth?

An individual with high self-esteem feels grounded. Have you heard the expression, 'a tree with strong roots can survive a fierce wind'? A person who has a strong base of self-worth feels balanced, aligned and better equipped to deal with challenges thrown at them in their life's journey. When an individual feels comfortable in their own skin they are authentic and genuine. This grounded personality possesses strength that builds resilience. Like the tree with strong roots, an individual who genuinely likes and respects who they are can weather the most turbulent times.

Is your driving force firing you up?

Fire is a powerful way to express a person's burning desire. Fire can burn at a frighteningly fast pace and as flames become bigger the heat becomes more intense. In people we translate this as having a dynamic and powerful energy. Often if the fire in a person's belly is too intense for too long they may experience burnout. Often emotions can be seen as hot or cold. For example, anger is usually seen as a hot emotion – 'he's hot-headed today' – whereas someone described as serene is seen as cool and composed. Passion is a hot emotion that can burn brightly and intensely yet can fade and cool quickly. The properties of fire perfectly describe the attribute of a strong driving force.

Do you allow your emotions to go with the flow?

Water can ebb and flow: sometimes the currents are strong; sometimes a river runs deep. Swimming against the current or the tide can be stressful and arduous. In the same way, the range of emotions people experience through the course of their lives guides their behaviour. Anger can move fluidly into sadness as our emotional reactions respond to the thoughts we are thinking. Heightened sensory awareness of emotional undercurrents within ourselves and others means we begin to understand what's going on under the surface. Bruce Lee explained water as a thing that can penetrate the hardest substance in the world, yet it's difficult to grasp with our hands. This sounds like a perfect description of our emotions.

Visioning from thin air

The next time you meet a person with a strong and compelling vision, notice how often their eyes look upwards – this really is blue-sky thinking in action. Air has been a symbol of vision with astrologists for centuries. Birds enjoy the freedom of the sky as their aerial perspective changes what they can envision. Gaining a bird's eye view suggests an elevated position that enables the viewer to survey a much wider landscape. I also like the metaphor of breathing pure, fresh air because we all share it – it truly is universal. Within an organisational context, the breath of each employee will collectively breathe life into a corporate vision.

The energy of a free spirit

Spirit is the fifth universal law of nature – an invisible, intangible and separate realm of existence that interfaces with the physical world. In her groundbreaking book *The Field*, investigative journalist Lynne McTaggart (2001) cites numerous scientific studies to prove that our environment is a pulsating power of consciousness – a non-material world of thought. Like energy. People with high energy levels tend to be in good spirits, positive and more collaborative. Energy is invisible, intangible, yet everything affects it and it affects everything.

The Symbol of Star Quality

The Symbol of Star Quality depicts the five pillars of charisma blended with the symbolic representations of the universal laws of nature. At first glance it may remind you of Leonardo da Vinci's Vitruvian Man who juxtaposes the human body as a star within a pentagram shape. He beautifully illustrates the symmetry of the human body and how we extend and align to the universe as a whole. Da Vinci's drawing holds some interesting theories about the universe because it epitomises power, alignment and the flow of perfection. The state of charisma is when we have attained balance in each of the five pillars so that we operate in a state of flow, a peak performing state that is supported by the laws of nature. This symbol also illustrates that the five pillars activate and are aligned with two powerful principles: first, that of being authentically true to who you are at your core (the real you) and, second, the level of purpose and meaning your life holds for you.

Relating the Symbol of Star Quality to business leaders

How does the Symbol of Star Quality relate to business leaders of the past and present? Once you are familiar with working with these five pillars it becomes easy to identify in others which pillars are enhancing or preventing their charisma from flourishing.

Sir Richard Branson, founder of Virgin Group

Richard Branson is a serial entrepreneur with an astonishingly impressive track record for taking risks that few other business leaders would contemplate. His ventures portray creativity, insight and a desire to do something that makes him feel proud, and this combination of vision and authenticity builds his charismatic leadership style. Branson left school without any A levels and has built his business empire from scratch. His vision has created the cross-fertilisation of the Virgin brand in many types of products and services. Yet his pioneering vision into space tourism with Virgin Galactic places him in a different league to other visionary business leaders. Sir Richard Branson's ability to connect emotionally is summed up by one of his own quotes, 'You can't be a good leader if you don't genuinely like people' (CBS, 2007). Despite his wealth he is humble, down-to-earth and has been known to serve drinks to passengers on Virgin Atlantic flights. People like and warm to him. His self-esteem attribute appears to be strong because he is happy to appear in ads and TV programmes and be at the receiving end of jokes and gentle mickey-taking. His driving force was strengthened early in his life when it is reported that at the age of six his mother shoved him out of the car and told him to make his own way home. It's little wonder that massive goals that appear unachievable to everyone else simply excite and energise Richard.

Maria Eva Duarte de Peron (Evita)

Eva Peron transcended a life of poverty to become Argentina's Lady of Hope in 1945 when she married Juan Peron who became president a year after they were married. She had a major influence on the lives of millions of 20th-century Argentinians. Throughout her short life she was extremely driven, a trait that was softened by her ability to connect with the people of Argentina. Eva was a skilled speaker. When she spoke she used ordinary yet emotive language that allowed her support and empathy for her own class to inspire high levels of trust and devotion. In 1945 Colonel Juan Peron was arrested by a group of military men who did not support his political views. When Eva spoke she radiated energy, passion and enthusiasm. These attributes enabled her to persuade 50,000 trade union supporters to march in protest for Peron's release. Her vision proved to be a catalyst for change in her campaign for equal rights when she founded an organisation to distribute wealth to the poor. The only attribute that was not as well developed within Eva Peron was her self-esteem. She needed to lavish huge amounts of money on Christian Dior dresses, fur coats and jewellery for herself. This was her way of building her worth. She could also be cruel when faced with anyone who disagreed with her. Sometimes the biggest dictators are hiding huge insecurities about not feeling good enough.

Boris Johnson, Mayor of London

Boris Johnson, Mayor of London, effortlessly manages to grab the headlines whereas David Cameron's press and media team would pay good money for his vote-winning charm. Research in 2013 by YouGov, whose findings are drawn from people in politics, business, media, academia and the public sector, found that Boris Johnson is the only leading politician to score positively with how they are doing in their current roles. Boris is one of those rare characters who is irresistible in front of the camera because he is maverick and completely authentic. Compared to the horde of straight-laced politicians who will make you want to throw something at your television if they go on too long, he oozes charisma in his bumbling, buffoon-like way that makes him entertainment gold. He's also one of those rare politicians that successfully reaches out across the political divide. Until he became Mayor of London, the Conservatives had been hammered by Ken Livingstone in the mayoral elections, but Boris produced a big swing in his favour in 2008 and then went on to keep his position as Mayor of London despite his party being hit hard in the local elections. Whilst many politicians these days appear to be little more than party yes-men and women, Boris hasn't been afraid to forge his own path and at times publicly disagree with David Cameron. Politicians can sometimes appear 'out of touch' so Johnson's ability to show his warmth and humanness scores highly with the electorate. When Boris Johnson speaks at Conservative Party conferences he is an authentic star, who lights up every room he enters. He makes people laugh and feel good.

Barack Hussein Obama, 44th US president

The electorate generally respond positively to charismatic politicians because they are good at winning the hearts of voters. Yet there is a wariness around politicians because they are not always viewed as socially responsible. Looking back over every US presidential election since TV became widespread, the apparently more charismatic candidate has won. Barack Hussein Obama II is the 44th President of the United States and the first African American to hold this office. His most prominent personal attributes are confidence, assertiveness and congeniality. In office, the behaviour of confident, ambitious leaders like Obama is characteristically shaped by their self-belief, suggesting high levels of self-esteem. Because of this extraordinary confidence in his own ideas and his potential to create a vision of success for his country's future, Obama's charisma increases in direct proportion to his beliefs. He is at his best when he is campaigning for what he truly believes in, highlighting the impact that authenticity plays in charismatic appeal. He delivers powerful speeches that evoke high levels of emotion from his audience that keeps them mesmerised throughout. When travelling abroad, Obama is conciliatory, humble and apt to listen before speaking. He intuitively knows how to convey empathy and the nation's mood. His strong driving force means that he does not shy away from challenges. In today's economy, political leaders that have the ability to blend emotional communication with intellectual prowess create the biggest impact on electoral followership.

Steve Jobs, co-founder Apple Computers

On the day he died, people everywhere flocked to Apple Stores in a sort of mass pilgrimage that could be likened to the way the British public reacted to Princess Diana's death. This extraordinary man's vision and powerful driving force came at the expense of his sensory awareness and compassion. There are stories about his cruel denials over the paternity of his daughter, the long working hours Apple employees were expected to put in and the conditions at his factory sites. Key personnel describe how working at Apple destroyed marriages and how they experienced excessive stress levels because of the dictatorial demands and high standards of perfection that Jobs expected everyone to adhere to. One of his documented quotations highlights his vision and obsession with perfectionism:

> My job is to not be easy on people. My job is to make them better. My job is to pull things together from different parts of the company and clear the ways and get the resources for the key projects. And to take these great people we have and to push them and make them even better, coming up with more aggressive visions of how it could be.

> *Fortune Magazine*, March 2008

Yet paradoxically people who worked for him and openly suffered under his leadership still felt a strong emotional connection with him. In terms of his energy, Steve Jobs knew how to work a crowd. He could build excitement that garnered significant media attention. He was a showman at product launches and displayed real flair for 'the big reveal'. No other Apple executive has been able to generate this level of media interest. Ultimately he was a man with a purpose – he told the *Wall Street Journal* (1993), 'Going to bed at night saying we've done something wonderful… that's what matters to me.'

– CHARISMA ENHANCER –

How much of your charismatic potential are you using? You can access a complimentary version of my Charisma Profiling Tool on nikkijowen.com/freeminiprofile This will show you what percentage of your own charismatic potential you are currently using. Then you'll see which of the five pillars require your attention for developing your charisma.

Chapter 4

——

Survival or growth

Human beings naturally search for a symbolic order of the universe – a sense of coherence, continuity and justice. As individuals, we unconsciously connect and feel safe with a leader who we perceive will bring order to the chaos of ordinary living. According to the distinguished sociologist Edward Shils (1965), 'the charismatic leader seems to be connected to the transcendental powers of the universe and is able to re-establish a sense of order in his followers'. Sigmund Freud supports this view by examining the impact of our upbringing. During the initial stages of a child's development, the infant is not able to experience or perceive any difference between themselves and their external reality. Until taught differently, the child believes that *they are the entire universe*. With time, the child begins to understand that their mother, whom they perceive as a powerful influence, is a *separate* entity. However, the child maintains a sense of its own power when their mother responds to their demands. Gradually, the child's frustrations grow as they experience that their needs are not always immediately satisfied by 'the universe' and, at a certain point in their development, they discover the cruel truth that they are not omnipotent at all. Yet because of earlier infant *perceptions*, the desire to return to this feeling of power and connectedness remains, burning strongly within the child and then the adult, throughout their life. One very effective way of feeling connected and aligned with this internal power is to identify oneself with someone who is perceived as powerful – a charismatic leader. When we feel connected we induce a deep internal feeling of safety. We are programmed from birth to follow or to be followed. Leadership guru Simon Sinek (2014) explains that our genetic programming means that when we feel sure that a leader will keep us safe, we will march behind them and work tirelessly to see their visions come to life and proudly call ourselves their followers. A charismatic leader has the power and ability to speak directly to the hearts of individuals so they feel safe and secure in the knowledge they will be protected by their leader. Yet for a leader to access their true charismatic potential, they too have to feel safe.

A cellular reaction

The ability to feel safe and to create a place of safety is helped by understanding what happens to us at a cellular level. Biologists estimate that there are in excess of 70 trillion cells in our body. Stem cell biologist Dr Bruce Lipton discovered that our genes do not control our biology. Initially he experimented by removing the nucleus, the perceived command centre of a cell, in the expectation that it would die. This didn't happen. Instead what Dr Lipton discovered was that the cells' *perception of their environment* determines how the genes are expressed. The formation of a cell is dictated by its environment – this process is epigenetics. Each cell in your body can only ever function in one of two operating mechanisms. Survival or growth. Imagine you are feeling stressed about a project at work. Your body releases three main hormones into your system: adrenalin, norepinephrine and cortisol. Your cells immediately sense toxins in the environment and the gates on the surface of every cell in your body close, creating a vacuum that blocks out all the toxins.

Whilst this method of cellular protection works effectively for a short period of time, if the cells' gates remain closed they are preventing the absorption of valuable proteins that are vital for cellular growth. If you deprive anything of nourishment for too long it will eventually die. Imagine a castle under siege. With its drawbridge pulled up and thick protective walls the enemy's attack will fail to penetrate the castle's walls. If the attacking army decides to wait, after a while the supplies of food and water within the castle will eventually run out and the occupants inside the 'protective' walls become vulnerable and likely to succumb to attack. This is why people who experience long-term stress start to get ill as their immune system weakens. Stress is killing vast quantities of their cells and their body is unable to replace them.

The biology behind organisational silos

Nearly every system in the human body exists to help us to survive and thrive. If we sense danger our defences go up. If we feel safe among the people within our organisation, we relax and are more open to trust and cooperation. Charismatic leaders recognise that the quickest way to achieve high performance is when the organisation's culture is collaborative. Whilst processes and managerial acumen are important they do not create safety. They do not win the 'hearts' of employees. Showing people how to perform their job is not the only factor required to ensure high performance.

People need to know why they are performing their job so that their hearts become invested with the organisation's success.

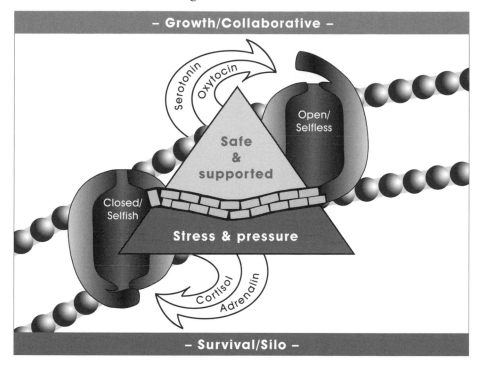

The damage of feeling isolated

In her interview for *Panorama* with Martin Bashir, the late Princess Diana stated, 'There is no better way to dismantle a personality than to isolate it.' Feelings of isolation cause people to close down emotionally and erect a protective wall around themselves. Within an organisational context individual or departmental silos are perpetuated when employees are afraid to approach other departments, and occur in companies where the leadership is ineffective. Collaboration is a vital component to business success. Yet many organisations consciously and unconsciously promote a culture that creates barriers to cooperation. Silo thinking is damaging to companies because it promotes closed thinking, stagnates growth and leads to poor decisions. Typically employee engagement will suffer and this ultimately impacts on the bottom line. The key to understanding how to dismantle silos lies once again in our cellular biology. When we feel under pressure and start to experience a stressful state, our body releases cortisol and adrenaline. This causes cells to seal themselves and move into a protective operating mechanism. Cells become closed silos that prevent other growth hormones from entering them. Alternatively, when we feel safe and supported we release serotonin (a chemical that makes us feel good) and oxytocin (a chemical that stimulates trust and empathy) that decreases stress responsiveness and increases our openness towards social belonging. This chemical reaction opens the cell gates so they can absorb nutrients for growth. In other words, an environment where individuals feel stressed will *actively encourage* selfish behaviour, closed thinking and a silo mentality. A safe and supportive environment will *actively encourage* selfless behaviour, an open attitude towards change and teamwork and a collaborative and caring culture. When people have to manage perceived dangers from inside their organisation, the organisation itself becomes less able to face the dangers from outside. When people feel a need to protect themselves from their colleagues, the whole organisation suffers. But when trust and cooperation thrive internally, people pull together and the organisation grows stronger as a result.

– CHARISMA ENHANCER –

Listen with your heart. There is a real difference in the way that people listen to you. Some people listen to you to 'catch you out' and entrap you or they listen with the sole purpose of finding an angle to put their own viewpoint. Yet someone who listens with compassion, perception and genuine interest without any hidden agenda will create a feeling of warmth, safety and connectivity. According to Nancy Kline (1999), author of *Time to Think*, the quality of our listening will determine the quality of the other person's response. Sometimes, people just need to talk. It is incredibly therapeutic to be able to express what you really feel inside.

Epigenetics and environmental factors

The hippocampus is the part of the brain responsible for short-term and long-term memory. Scientists know that it affects the epigenome, which is the chemical compound around a gene thread that affects which genes are expressed. Environmental influences, such as a person's diet, exposure to pollutants and emotions affect gene function, protein production and human health. It's a flexible system that responds to the environment. Two people hardwired for the same trait might not show that trait in the same way because they have differences that either mute or emphasise the genes. The epigenome plays an important role in controlling stress hormones, including cortisol, which is released by the adrenal gland when the brain and body react to perceived danger. This means that peoples' perceptions create differentiation at a cellular level that determines whether they operate in survival or growth mode. If the environment and culture of our place of work is safe, harmonious and happy, more employees will find it easier to operate from a growth mindset, helping their organisation to achieve more, even with less available resources. If the environment is based on a culture of fear then this will unwittingly trigger a survival mindset.

Two types of survival responses

When threatened, an animal will either run away or start to attack. When we feel unsafe, our instinctive reaction tends to trigger two different categories of behaviour. We either erect an invisible wall of protection around us and withdraw emotionally into ourselves – this is often referred to as 'flight' or 'going into our cave', and mimics what happens to us at a cellular level. Or, we may lash out with excessive emotional intensity as we unconsciously try to hurt our perceived attacker so that we feel more powerful – this is our 'fight' response. The ability to identify whether an employee is operating from a survival mechanism is hugely beneficial when it comes to determining the best way to communicate, manage and lead them.

– Indicators of survival and growth –		
Survival ('flight')	Survival ('fight')	Growth
Mistakes from someone who is usually efficient and reduced productivity	Political and/or yes-man/woman mentality/back-stabbing/focus on what others are doing wrong	Focus on others, their team, colleagues and organisation
Closed minded, negative and procrastinates	Stiff shouldered and upward slant to chin (defiance and holding it together)	Shares and invites ideas
Workaholic and focused on work-related tasks at the exclusion of other life areas	Angry, irritable, aggressive, quick to blame others	High performer; takes ownership

– Indicators of survival and growth –		
Survival ('flight')	Survival ('fight')	Growth
Getting through the day and constant clock watching	Headaches/ lower back pain and neck problems	Displays creative thinking
Just do their job – don't proactively give an opinion	Nervous habits: pacing/nail biting/compulsive talking	Contributes at meetings and invites feedback/ contributions from others
Sleeping too much	Memory loss and poor concentration	Good active listener and displays empathy
Recent weight gain (particular around waist and hips)/comfort eating/ junk food/addictions or recent weight loss	Bad recall of facts	Walks tall with expanded chest as if the person's heart is leading them
Round shouldered (carrying the weight of the world) and hunched	Critical and nitpicking	Appears relaxed and in good physical shape
Negative language: 'these things always happen to me'	Not sleeping/inability to relax	Appears to be 'in a state of flow' and 'in the zone'
Worried about making a mistake/what can go wrong	Heart palpitations and high blood pressure	Reacts positively to change
Reluctance to help others – appear insular, lonely and isolated	Overly driven/pushy and manic	Good team player and communicates freely
Social withdrawal/stressed and appears out of control or cries frequently/emotional	Explosive angry outbursts	High balanced energy, relaxed, appreciative and calm
Tired/minor illnesses ranging from colds, coughs, spots, dull skin/hair (immune system switches off)	Actively seeks to sabotage and find co-saboteurs	Smiles regularly, can laugh at self and learns from mistakes
Short-term sick days	Uncharacteristically loud and commanding voice tonality	Deeply intuitive, emotionally intelligent and sensory aware
Feeling overwhelmed by demands from the business	Appears out of control	Engaged – works with 100 per cent commitment and goes beyond the expected
Apathy, low energy, monotone, shallow breathing, soaks up other people's energy	Impatient and rude	Possesses a 'can do' attitude/ empowered, confident

Maslow's hierarchy of needs

This survival or growth cellular reaction is a microcosm for what is happening to our multicellular system – our body. According to Maslow's hierarchy of needs, there are five basic levels of needs that we move through: 1. physiological, 2. safety, 3. love and belonging, 4. esteem and 5. self-actualisation. If you're hungry, you find it difficult to concentrate. If you are scared, your immediate motivation is to escape the source of your fear. If you feel cold, then finding a way to get warm will drive your behaviour. The first two levels of Maslow's hierarchy of needs have to be satisfied before we can operate in a growth mindset. If an employee is worried about their job or has an abusive and controlling boss, that employee will automatically shut down at a cellular level and operate in survival mode. This will impact on their relationships with colleagues and their aptitude for becoming a team player (level 3 – love and belonging). Their feeling of uncertainty about their future is not helped with factors designed for growth-based levels like recognition or a different job title (level 4 – esteem needs) because these 'motivators' can only be appreciated when that individual is in a growth mindset. The top levels of Maslow's hierarchy of needs, belonging, esteem and self-actualisation, indicate that the individual is in a growth mindset. Desirable attributes and behaviours, such as being visionary, feeling engaged, and being creative and innovative, can only happen when an individual is in growth, regardless of whether that individual is an employee or a leader. These distinctions between survival and growth mindsets consequently determine the best way to interact with each individual. When employees are operating in a mindset of survival, any attempt to utilise growth-based motivators will produce a reaction of lethargy or, even more likely, resistance.

Behaviours that create safety and collaboration

Understanding Maslow's hierarchy of needs means that to initially stimulate and then fulfil the need to belong – an essential part of collaboration – the organisation through its leadership team needs to ensure that individuals can transcend Maslow's two survival levels to activate their internal biology of growth. Therefore the starting point for the charismatic leader is to create a safe environment that stimulates a growth mindset and a culture of collaboration. This naturally empowers others to perform at their full potential. There are recognisable leadership behaviours that when demonstrated will serve to either build fear or create safety.

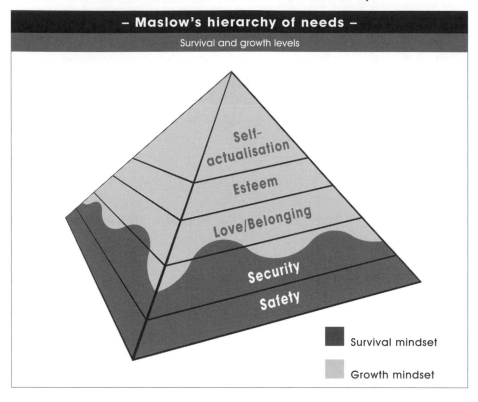

Leadership behaviours that create fear/silos/ selfish responses	Leadership behaviours that create safety/ collaboration/selfless responses
Indecision, particularly during tough times	Speaks truthfully and is honest
Casts blame on others	Respects others viewpoint
Competitive and ruthless	Reliable and trustworthy
Critical and judgemental	Seeks to understand
Sacrifices 'heart' count for 'head' count efficiency	Sacrifices 'theirs' for 'ours'
Puts own interests first	Puts own interests aside to protect others
Rewards individual performance	Rewards team performance
Managerial acumen	Leadership excellence
Takes care of profits first	Takes care of people first

Daring to lose to win

In 2002, when Sven-Göran Eriksson became manager of the England football team he believed that football matches were not won with training and tactics alone but with the power of the mind. Sven knew that if players played defensively (or in other words from a mindset of survival), whilst they might not lose, they would not create opportunities to win. Taking a shot at goal weakens the team's defence so every shot at goal is a risk for that player. Supported by Professor Willi Railo from the University of Oslo, Sven identified that when players experienced stress around fear of failure or fear of making mistakes, their performance suffered. This fear of failure has become known as choking – a crippling form of anxiety and a negative reaction to the huge burden of expectation. Players become inhibited, take fewer risks and consequently underachieve. This is often witnessed during penalty shoot-outs, when the mental pressure causes competent players to kick the ball badly. Sven and Professor Railo created a team mantra – *You have to dare to lose to win.* If players feel secure in the knowledge that if their shot at goal fails they will not receive any negative consequences. The burden of 'screwing up' is then lifted. Sven's calm manner during vital matches demonstrated to the players that he was not afraid of failure. He encouraged his players to take risks. He didn't criticise them for making mistakes. Ultimately, if a football player feels secure then he performs better. In fact in the world of sport 'mistakes' are viewed as practice.

Creating a safe environment

When employees don't feel safe for any reason they often appear withdrawn, resistant, disinterested and even incompetent. Yet they are scared. Their body is in a state of survival and has effectively shut down. Their fear chokes their ability to think clearly and perform effectively. In this situation, leaders have to give priority to creating a safe environment. On numerous occasions I have witnessed the way senior leadership teams react to presentations and proposals for new improved ways of doing things from their employees. On the surface they encourage idea generation yet will criticise and pull apart ideas that do not instantly grab their attention. This creates fear. In time employees become truly reluctant to think outside the box because of the potential humiliation of having their ideas attacked so publicly. How can you build engagement if people are afraid? I remember being invited onto the sales floor of a well-known organisation and witnessed the sales director screaming abuse at some poor individual sat at the other side of the floor. This created fear and tension across the whole sales floor and immediately choked the telesales teams' performance. When I was pioneering my approach to developing charismatic leadership, one of the early adopters – a global publishing company – had discovered a mobile phone app that would make the sound of a whip being cracked. Within days this app had gone viral amongst leaders and managers who openly bragged about the fear this app created within their teams. Often, leaders are so driven by their desire to get the result they are oblivious to how their people are responding. Fear as a motivational tactic might work in the short term, yet it cannot sustain high performance in the longer term. This is why sensory awareness and heartfelt communication is a vital requisite for a charismatic leader.

– CHARISMA ENHANCER –

When communicating with someone in survival, show your vulnerability because you are non-verbally demonstrating that there is nothing to fear if they speak from their own authentic self. The ability to be vulnerable is a huge strength. Dolf van den Brink was just 36 when he became the chief executive of Heineken USA. In a revealing interview given to the *New York Times* (26 November 2013) he advocates that the number one thing that generates trust is vulnerability. To be vulnerable can bring amazing and unexpected positive reactions, insights and assistance because it exposes elements and information that would otherwise remain closed or hidden.

Proactive and reactive

There are two types of people in this world: those who are proactive and those who are reactive. The fundamental difference between the two is whether they are operating in survival or growth. Proactive people are 'towards pleasure' motivated. These people will consider the risk of failure of a particular course of action, weigh it up against the potential and imagined pleasure that success would bring them, and will then commit wholeheartedly to doing whatever it is that they need to do to achieve their desired outcome. Ultimately this unconscious programming creates growth at a cellular level. Reactive people, by contrast, are motivated by 'away from pain'. Only when the level of discomfort within their existing situation becomes intolerable (and very often not until somebody else has made this decision for them) will reactive people be forced to take action. They will consider the risk of failure of a particular course of action, and then weigh it up against the additional and imagined pain that it would bring them if this new proposed action was to fail. This type of internal and often unconscious programming stimulates a deep cellular reaction of survival. It is not surprising then, that reactive people are far more likely to procrastinate and become stuck before reluctantly 'proceeding with caution' rather than 'committing wholeheartedly'. Rather than attribute the trait of being proactive or reactive to personality, what if these traits are manifested as a direct result of the survival or growth operating mechanism?

Resilience is a growth mindset

So what's your 'strategy' at the moment of defeat? Have you ever analysed what actually goes on, within your mind and your body, at that precise moment when it dawns on you that it's all gone horribly wrong? What is it that you feel when the sky falls in, when all of your hopes and dreams come crashing down around you, and you realise that it was you who created this outcome, and it was you that made it happen? At that moment we allow ourselves to feel defeated, no matter whether we are fundamentally a proactive or a reactive person, our ability to imagine a positive outcome completely deserts us. In that split second when we realise that things have not gone the way that we had hoped, and visualised and planned, fear takes over. In the absence of a compelling vision and without huge amounts of self-belief, all the willpower in the world will not get us back up on our feet. We have allowed fear to choke our ability to think and perform effectively.

A compelling vision builds resilience

Charismatic leaders come into their own at those times when defeat is staring them down. Because against all odds the strength of their vision and the belief they possess about their ability (high self-esteem) enables them to perform from a growth mindset. This inner strength will create a feeling of safety in that leader's followers. When you think of the truly charismatic leaders throughout history, it is often difficult to separate the leader from the cause. Martin Luther King would not have been anywhere near as compelling and inspiring if he didn't 'have a dream' that he was brave enough, not just to share, but to demonstrate his unflinching commitment to. Charismatic leaders draw upon a compelling vision deep inside themselves that inspires and refuels the imagined pleasure within their followers, building a commitment to doing what needs to be done. At times of real adversity truly charismatic leaders will demonstrate an extraordinary instinct to reframe fear as an *opportunity*. Winston Churchill spoke eloquently about 'how we shall fight on the beaches, and on the landing grounds, and on the fields and the streets, and in the hills, and we shall never surrender'. In so doing he brilliantly paced the emotions of the nation and showed his own fearlessness to embolden the hearts of the British people. This is why charismatic people are more resilient. Their vision is so compelling that they literally cannot get it out of their mind. Their belief in their own ability to achieve their vision gives them the courage to 'feel the fear and do it anyway'. This constant and empowering mindset creates high levels of mental toughness and resilience because they rarely switch into a survival mindset.

Courage and charisma

Rampant fear has sent many organisational cultures into a downward spiral, particularly during economic downturns where the tenuous state of the economy creates untold levels of anxiety. According to an annual survey report in 2012 by CIPD in partnership with Simplyhealth, two fifths of organisations reported an increase in stress-related absence over the previous year. Two fifths of public sector organisations and one fifth of private sector organisations were planning redundancies, which places further strain, fear and uncertainty on the workforce. In these situations, people tend to keep their heads down and their mouths shut in order to survive – yet survival chokes performance. These are the times that call for bold, confident, courageous leadership. History shows us repeatedly that those with the guts to step forward, take some risks and lead change during downturns will be the winners as the economy rebounds. When a leader of an organisation possesses courage it perpetuates a feeling of safety and security in others. The military have a tradition that leaders eat last because it demonstrates that they are prepared to sacrifice themselves for the welfare of their regiment. Joan of Arc won the loyalty of her soldiers because of her courage and her charisma. During that time, the military was a male subculture within which men in the military were jealously protective of their own elite status. Joan's ability to join the military should have been crippled three times over: by her young age (she was hardly more than a child), by the fact that she was a peasant in a feudal society and because she was female. Yet Joan's innate courage and her absence of any apparent fear were infectious and caused thousands of men to want to follow her. Nelson Mandela's life is a story of huge courage. He endured a 27-year imprisonment for his dream of a better and equal South Africa. Mandela said, 'I learned that courage was not the absence of fear, but the triumph over it... The brave man is not he who does not feel afraid, but he who conquers that fear' (2012). This man's vision was so completely and utterly compelling for him that he was prepared to stand by his beliefs in the face of devastating personal adversity for the benefit of equality amongst his people. Sir Ranulph Fiennes, arguably the world's greatest living explorer, showed incredible courage when faced with nature's most dangerous and difficult challenges. The elements vital to the success of Fiennes's expeditions included teamwork, courage, determination, resilience and the ability to perform under extreme pressure. His men felt safe under his watch and consequently performed their duties to a high level. For a charismatic leader working within a corporate environment, the very nature of their character and personality gives rise to a plethora of situations in which they require courage and steely nerves to pursue what they believe to be right. Courageous leaders can say difficult things and employees won't sense any fear about what may happen in the future. When leaders choose to 'keep a lid' on bad news, the uncertainty of what may or may not happen often causes more fear than the bad news. Courageous leadership requires people to see what others don't want to see, and do what others don't want to do. An organisation may have the ability to make the necessary changes, but it requires courageous leaders who possess strength, conviction and the stamina to hold on through the inevitable resistance.

Master your breathing technique. This is the quickest way to create an emotional and energetic change. Deep and slow breaths will lower your blood pressure, promote feelings of calm and quickly help you to access a state of relaxation. Within a business environment, it may not always be appropriate to suggest to others who are experiencing anxiety that they take some big deep breaths. If you are breathing in a balanced and controlled way the other person's breathing will naturally adjust to your breathing rate. From a physics perspective there is less energy used when two objects or systems are aligned with each other. Your body contains an autonomic mechanism that puts you in synch with strong, external rhythms, pulses or beats. This synchronisation is known as entrainment. If you are breathing deeply and calmly you influence the other person's breathing so you both breathe calmly, deeply and at the same time. Good calming breaths involve breathing from the abdomen, so your abdomen expands on the in breath, and exhaling through the mouth.

Chapter 5

Protective walls

I t is widely accepted that an organisation's success depends upon the people it employs. High performing employees will drive efficiency and profit upwards. The senior leadership team sets the tone for the culture of the organisation. The way that roles and responsibilities are defined will impact on the efficiency of processes implemented. Needs-based training and development programmes seek to improve overall competence and integrated communication strategies are designed to inform and educate. *These elements work well when employees are in growth.* But when employees are in survival they erect invisible and impenetrable walls to protect themselves. This disconnects them from other people; they emotionally detach from their team and disengage from the organisation. Consequently those employees in survival will not be influenced by the available resources or the traditional methods employed by their leader to engage and inspire them. Conventional tools or processes that work well when people are in growth will appear to be like shooting arrows into a concrete wall – they will simply bounce off and fall away. Nothing gets through. Irrespective of how accurately the archer has aimed their arrow, it will never penetrate the wall and never connect with the target. In the vast majority of cases, the stuff that stops people from reaching their full potential is not a lack of skill or a lack of knowledge. The barriers that block a person from performing well are driven by *a primal need to protect their core self.* Difficulties with personal relationships, money worries or health issues can trigger a survival mindset at work.

Walls are a survival strategy

An individual's programming from their past can create a survival mindset in the present moment. From a very young age, we learn how to 'put up walls' that protect us from harm, failure, embarrassment, hurt and a host of other negative experiences. Walls have been a part of our survival strategy for so long that we are often unaware that they are there and we may struggle to differentiate 'our wall' from 'our core self'. Even walls that we may be aware of can be hard to dismantle. Have you ever wanted to lose weight? Most people who want to lose weight fail. Not because they don't know what to do, what to eat or what not to eat to lose weight. Their willpower, or what they see as a lack of it, will sabotage their success.

Overeating is not about satisfying their appetite, it is about satisfying an emotional lack, a void within them. Overeating is often an effect of a programmed need to feel safe. Their 'wall' of protection is their excess weight. Only when their unconscious mind believes that it is safe to let go of their weight will they achieve sustainable weight loss. Willpower is when our conscious mind goes head to head with the core values, beliefs and programming that we hold within our unconscious mind. Because many of our walls are unconscious we end up working against ourselves. Part of you wants to lose weight and part of you believes that you have to finish what is on your plate because when you were growing up your parents repeatedly told you that *people in Africa are starving to death*.

Walls created in childhood

Many people's walls are not built during their time within the organisation where they work; they have brought their walls with them. Their early childhood programming will often create walls that conventional training will fail to penetrate. You have all the resources you need inside to achieve whatever you want and the quickest way to access these internal resources is by identifying and removing the walls or barriers you have built up over the years. Numerous studies highlight that 80 per cent of our behaviour is based on unconscious and negative programming from our past. Imagine that on the day of your birth you are given an iPod. It can't play any music because you have not had a chance to download any yet. As you begin your journey through life your brain is operating in the theta frequency, which means that you are in a hypnagogic, deep, trance-like state and are incredibly suggestible at this young age. We learn by observing, recording and downloading our information and programmes without any objective criteria in terms of 'this is good for me' or 'this is bad for me'. By the time you get to the age of six or seven you become more consciously aware and have managed to install thousands of programmes. As adults, many of our behaviours, decisions and actions are due to our programming as a child. During my own childhood my parents loved each other, yet had a volatile relationship. This meant lots of shouting and rows. As a little girl I believed that I had caused these rows and formed a belief that I was unlovable. I'm not blaming my parents for this belief, yet it created huge issues for me as an adult. I struggled with personal relationships, believing that if people knew the real me, they wouldn't like me, let alone love me. As a result I became a hyper fun-loving clown, a real dare devil, a show-off desperate to win approval. These were my walls triggered by a childhood belief. Your own negative programming, even if you are oblivious to it, will definitely be diluting your charisma. The reason many employees put up their protective walls is usually because one of their childhood programmes has been inadvertently triggered in the workplace.

Reacting as a seven-year-old

A software engineer working for a major financial institution was trying to improve his confidence during presentations. His voice would become very quiet and he struggled to project an air of credibility and charisma. His company had funded many courses for him and whilst they were interesting and helpful to a point, none of them helped to address his quiet voice tone and lack of confidence. His breakthrough moment came when he identified a previously suppressed memory from when he was seven, when he was being inappropriately reprimanded by his mother. At work, whenever he was 'put on the spot' he unwittingly responded as the humiliated seven-year-old. By working with his unconscious mind, this previously suppressed memory was uncovered and his voice became deeper and he began breathing from his abdomen instead of from his throat. He now finds it easy to speak out at meetings and express his point of view succinctly and with passion. The wall he created at seven had been affecting his professional career.

Traumatic events can create walls

The financial director of a housing association appeared extremely resistant and distant with his team. His attitude was having a negative impact on other members within the senior leadership team who found him to be unapproachable and intimidating. His 'wall' had been created at 17 when he had been badly beaten up in a completely unprovoked attack. His self-confidence had been literally knocked out of him. He still held onto the belief he formed at 17 – you can't trust anyone – and this was why he appeared distant and wary. When he felt safe to explore what was behind some of his behaviour he was able to acknowledge the impact of this event and understand that this belief was no longer relevant or appropriate to his life now. Recognising that the fear he felt was an old fear enabled him to feel safe and his wall disappeared. The entire senior leadership team noticed an immediate change in his attitude towards them.

Feeling safe softens walls of resistance

Walls are exhausting to keep in place. We try to present and maintain a facade to the outside world that is different to who we really are inside. Resistance and negativity are simply imposters of the real enemy – fear. When you feel safe, when someone really sees you, the real you, and you believe that they like the real you, this awakens an inner knowing that everything is better when you can express yourself freely. Julie works for a FTSE 100 company in the manufacturing sector. Despite being identified as talented her career had stagnated and career progression appeared to stall at final interview stage. Concerns were raised about her enthusiasm and passion for the new roles identified and peers who were initially perceived as less able were being promoted before her. Once Julie felt safe enough to open up and talk about her confusing emotions she identified feeling vulnerable when giving presentations. She 'saw' every future progression as having to deliver more presentations – even when this wasn't actually the case. The moment Julie understood what was blocking her, she enrolled on a presentations skills course and secured a promotion within five months. A charismatic leader has the ability to create a safe environment and a feeling of security that allows them to communicate beyond people's walls. Individuals feel safe to 'let down their guard'. When a leader is authentic, compassionate and sells a compelling vision that leader is able to remove psychological and emotional barriers to engagement, empowerment, high performance and growth.

Procrastination is a protective wall

Protective walls come in many shapes and sizes within a corporate environment. William was an easy-going sales director who had a tendency to procrastinate over decisions. In a fast-paced and challenging work environment, the slightest bit of extra pressure caused an emotional paralysis within. His self-esteem was continually battered by his harsh critical self-talk. From an early age he believed 'I'm not good enough' and as a result he was unconsciously rejecting his true authentic self. No wonder he found it difficult to make decisions – his core self would want to do one thing yet his self-talk would completely sabotage the perceived benefits of taking any decision in case it wasn't the right decision. Years of operating within an industry with a leader who had a low tolerance to mistakes and was quick to slash budgets and manpower to hit the bottom line at any cost caused William to feel continually afraid. William's wall was procrastination that was held in place by bricks of fear. When he began to respect, accept and listen to his true self he discovered how easy it became to make decisions that felt good. When he was headhunted for another position where he was working for a truly charismatic leader, he found it easy to make decisions. He felt safe, supported and valued.

Resistance is really fear in disguise

Maureen was an HR director with a reputation for being ruthless, intolerant and tough. She had a clipped voice tone that caused her to appear cold and insensitive. Whilst she openly accepted that she was naturally aloof I sensed a lack of desire to really change. Her working environment was very male-orientated and full of people who exhibited strong driver style behaviours. This caused her to close down emotionally to protect herself. Maureen had experienced several dysfunctional relationships – a couple of ex-husbands and a live-in boyfriend. Her new relationship had been brilliant initially yet was starting to feel toxic and destructive. She saw that the way she was dealing with people at work, particularly men, was similar to the way she dealt with her personal relationships. Because she had been repeatedly emotionally hurt in the past, whenever she felt attacked or challenged, her wall and all her defences were raised. As I helped her to feel safe, her heightened sensory awareness enabled her to pinpoint an event that caused this repeating pattern. Her first boyfriend suffered from manic depression and would sometimes fly into an unprovoked rage. One evening he lost his temper and jumped out of a window of their apartment. He was paralysed and confined to a wheelchair. It explained so much about her behaviour around men, particularly volatile men. Her relationships improved overnight. She recognised that her fear surrounding this traumatic event had unconsciously linked to the belief that men cause pain. This realisation resulted in her becoming warmer and more approachable at work.

Working in the wrong environment

Every employee is unique. Some will 'thrive' in your organisation; some will try to 'survive' in your organisation. If the individual is not suited to the environment within which they work they will create walls to enable them to cope. Paul was part of an executive management team for a utilities company. The top team were not working collaboratively and many of the monthly meetings resulted in personal attacks, professional rivalry and a judgemental attitude towards change. Paul was, at his core, a highly sensitive man who valued education, support and integrity. He had not fully appreciated how important it was to him to believe in what he was doing and respect the people he worked with. Once he recognised that his career values were not being satisfied in his current role he accepted a position within a university and instantly ignited his passion for helping others. In his new role he was regularly approached by fellow colleagues who found his sensitive and positive nature compelling.

Control freaks

You have probably encountered many people who, if you are being honest, could be described as 'control freaks' – indeed you may even describe yourself in this way. What I have found is that the need to control masks an overwhelming fear of feeling powerless. A successful leadership trainer working for a global organisation was continually exhausted and having trouble sleeping. He became more and more withdrawn and during meetings would often appear angry and attacking. His colleagues described him as bright, mentally sharp and 'a control freak' – he liked to have the last word on everything. When I first met him I found his behaviour was intimidating and aggressive. I instinctively knew that this was his wall. He was struggling to cope. As a child he had endured years of physical abuse from his mother that had resulted in his mother's imprisonment. The trauma and stress that he had buried for years (he admitted to never crying) was finally released in an intense and emotional way. His walls that had been built as a small boy took huge amounts of energy to keep them in place. He was terrified about losing control. Being able to grieve and express his deep sorrow for what he had endured meant he released years of pent up negative emotions. With these emotions gone he no longer had a need to hide behind protective walls and his energy surged. He accepted his past and consequently he began to radiate an inner sense of calm.

Creating a place of safety

You don't need a sledgehammer to break down people's walls. In fact, if people feel you are attacking their walls they will strengthen their defences. Imagine someone is trying to push you over – what do you do? Most people stiffen up and brace themselves to resist the pushing. This physical reaction also happens emotionally. People need to feel safe with you. When you have high levels of rapport and a connection that goes deeper than a superficial one, people begin to trust that you have their interests at heart. Only when this trust and connection has formed will the individual feel ready to communicate from their heart as opposed to from their protective walls.

Questions that soften people's walls

The words you speak are surface utterances, yet many words in your vocabulary are linked to emotions and other thoughts. Whenever you speak or whenever you don't speak you are communicating. Your ability to use language in a way that shifts an individual's perception of their world in a positive way will inspire and engage that individual. When you frame your language into a question format then the emphasis of response is placed with the individual. If your question helps them to notice what is missing from their perception of things then you naturally expand their horizon. For example, if an individual has a belief that they are not likeable and you ask them what qualities they like about themselves, they have to think in a different way just to respond to your question. The types of questions you ask hold the potential to reprogramme people's automatic and unhelpful patterns of thinking that has kept their walls in place. Questions that expand the other person's perceptions facilitate an opportunity to move from their stuck or unhelpful viewpoints. When this happens the individual will notice that their old viewpoint has changed shape and this automatically stimulates different thoughts, emotions, options and choices. I call these types of questions shapeshifting questions because you can cause a change in the shape of the problems and unhelpful perceptions held by others.

Shaping negatives into positives

When you can help an individual to connect with more positive thoughts then you are able to shift the way they feel. Because our reality is processed through the limited spectrum of our physical senses our perceptions are always inaccurate and incomplete. If the individual is only processing negative information, then questions that switch their awareness onto positive information will instantly change their view of the world, their emotional responses and also their energy.

Negative perception	Shapeshifting question
'I don't like the way he treats us'	So what do you respect about him?
'She's useless and incompetent'	What aspect of her job does she do well?
'I've really struggled with this change'	What have you learned from this?
'He really hurt me'	What was the positive intention behind his actions?
'She's not a team player'	If she was, what could she bring to our team?
'This whole experience has been a nightmare'	How has this experience shaped your character?

Looking with fresh eyes

When you experience your life through someone else's eyes your experience of your life changes. When you see your problem through the eyes of someone else you create an emotional detachment. Questions that enable individuals to see through the eyes of someone else will give them some objectivity that may change the shape of their current thinking.

Own perception	Shapeshifting question
'I just don't know what to do about this'	If this was my issue, what advice would you give me right now?
'She makes me feel so angry'	How do you think she's feeling about you right now?
'Their behaviour is really erratic'	If you were behaving erratically, what would you be feeling?
'He is very withdrawn'	If you were his best friend what would you want to do to help him?

Questions that empower

When an individual believes that they are 100 per cent responsible for what they are creating in their life, then they are living their life *at cause*. Many people tend to live a large portion of their lives *at effect* and blame others or circumstances for what they have not achieved in their life. People who are *at effect* see themselves as victims with no choices and this creates a feeling of powerlessness guaranteed to hold a protective wall in place. The roots of powerlessness are created in people's minds. By asking questions that presuppose that the individual is the *cause of their situation*, their thinking is immediately empowered.

'At effect' statement	Shapeshifting question
'The economy is the reason for our profit shortfall'	When did you decide to believe this about the economy?
'He's really aggressive with me and I feel unappreciated'	How is your emotional response to him impacting on his behaviour?
'This is the third team leader that's not worked out for us'	What's the common link between these three team leaders?
'She gets very defensive with feedback'	Is this her issue or yours?
'He just can't be bothered; his attitude sucks'	How would you need to change your behaviour to change his behaviour?

Dismantling walls leads to high performance

TED Talks sensation Simon Sinek explains that by cultivating a strong Circle of Safety where the focus is put first on morale ensures that high performance will follow. Walls within everyone, including you and your employees, block high performance. Resistance is not a chosen reaction by the other person; it is an unconscious reaction to fear and a primal need to seek protection. Only when the individual feels safe will they dismantle and soften their walls. To create a feeling of safety in others requires the charismatic leader to demonstrate compassion and strength in equal measure.

– CHARISMA ENHANCER –

Think of a time in your own life when you were operating in survival mode. What behaviours did you demonstrate to protect yourself during this time? How did others respond to these behaviours? What walls do you currently have? What keeps them in place? What situations soften your wall?

What purpose does your wall serve? Are your walls appropriate and valid for you now in the present moment?

Chapter 6

The Charisma Model

The Charisma Model blends the five pillars from the Symbol of Star Quality (see Chapter 3) with the survival and growth operating mechanisms. This illustrates the process required to dismantle the walls of resistance that build a collaborative and engaged culture.

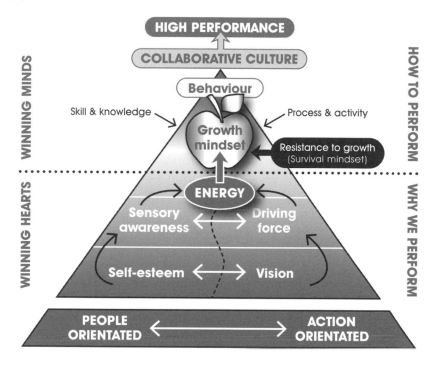

Changing behaviour

Creating a sustainable behavioural change in ourselves or other people is really arduous unless you influence and shape that individual's attitude. Imagine a balloon in a box. As the balloon inflates, the available space inside the box is reduced. Now imagine that the balloon represents a person's positive attitude and the space in the box represents resistance. The more space inhabited by the positive attitude reduces the available space for resistance. If there is very little positivity then the resistance will expand to fill the available space. The Charisma Model recognises that a positive attitude creates the optimum conditions for growth because it encourages cellular switching from survival to growth. Training and development programmes are significantly more effective when people want to learn. Processes become more efficient when people are motivated by a genuine desire to be the best they can be. The culture within the organisation will become collaborative when employees let down their walls and begin to support each other. When leaders concentrate on creating a safe environment and building a positive, growth mindset, the organisation's resources are optimised. Charismatic leaders achieve this by recognising that the same five internal pillars that determine their charismatic impact are equally relevant when working to help others improve their overall performance.

Self-esteem

When compared to people with low self-esteem, there is convincing evidence that people with high self-esteem are happier, as well as more likely to undertake difficult tasks and persevere in the face of failure. This is why some people are more resilient than others. High self-esteem means you hold yourself in high regard, whereas low self-esteem can be the cause of depression and a host of other problems.

Having a good self-esteem is essential, because:

- It helps you to feel good about yourself and feel good about what you do.
- It translates into belief in yourself, giving you the courage to try new things.
- It allows you to respect and honour yourself, even when you make mistakes.
- When you respect yourself, others will respect you too.
- You know that you're smart enough to make your own decisions and find it easier to make decisions. (Procrastination is often the result of a lack of confidence and low self-worth.)
- When you honour yourself, you make choices that nourish your mind and body enabling you to prioritise your emotional and physical health.

Someone with good self-esteem *feels comfortable in their own skin*. They appear confident and genuine because they are relaxed about showing others who they really are. The Mayor of London, Boris Johnson, is a man comfortable with himself. He effortlessly adapts to the diverse range of people he meets, yet regardless of the context or situation he remains true to himself. If you value and respect yourself, you know that there is a lot to like about you, so why try and hide it?

Charisma is contextual

Self-esteem (either the presence of it or the absence of it) is the primary reason why charisma is contextual. Your level of confidence increases or decreases based on how comfortable you are feeling. An individual who is confident in one job role may feel withdrawn in a different job role even if the duties are similar. I work mainly with business leaders from different industry sectors. Even though I encounter numerous challenging and controlling personality types, this is an arena I feel comfortable in – I am confident in this context. I remember being asked by David Hyner, a wonderful professional speaker, if I would share my personal story with 100 young teenagers. I was absolutely petrified! My confidence and I suspect my charisma deserted me – it was one of the most challenging moments of my entire career. The context change from business to secondary school affected my level of confidence. Marilyn Monroe, the iconic Hollywood movie star, could walk unnoticed down the street when she wasn't being filmed or photographed yet in front of a camera her legendary charisma and sex appeal shone brightly. Robbie Williams, the charismatic ex-boy band member of Take That, is excruciatingly shy when not performing. Former Prime Minister Gordon Brown performed badly in the 2010 live election debates because he felt insecure about being pitted against two younger adversaries. In an effort to compensate for his insecurities he was aggressive and bullish and turned off the electorate. Yet on the day he resigned as prime minister his speech to the press was incredibly moving and his genuine appeal shone through.

Sensory awareness

If an individual doesn't feel good enough they filter their reality in a way that perceives feedback as an implied criticism or threat. They may 'see' slights on their character and interpret a question as feeling under attack. If we feel threatened our automatic response is to protect ourselves, yet protective walls dampen and distort a person's awareness of self and others. A leader's level of emotional intelligence has a direct impact on their ability to create engagement. People who are expressive and compelling are in touch with their emotions and uninhibited about showing them. How can you evoke a strong emotional reaction within others if you are not able to engage your own emotions? Today, with the explosion of emotional intelligence, leaders operating from a solid base of logic are keen to develop their more intuitive side. Fascinating research in 1997 by Mayer and Salovey found that many organisational failures and problems were attributed to leaders lacking emotional skills. You may recall the emotional insensitivity of former BP chief executive Tony Hayward who decided to go racing on his yacht while his company struggled to contain 60,000 barrels of oil pouring into the Gulf of Mexico. He was completely out of touch with the thousands of people affected by the disaster (2010). With high levels of self-awareness you tune in to your emotional guidance system. Your emotions are continually giving you feedback about whether you are living your life in or out of alignment with your core authentic self. If you are not able to connect emotionally then you hamstring your receptivity to your environment.

Living in the moment

Being present, adopting a state of acceptance and going with the flow increase your sensory awareness and reduces stress. People respond better to people who are fully present. Your perception of another individual can hinder or help every interaction you have with them. Energy flows where your attention goes. When you focus all your attention on another person they feel energised and valued. Listening without judgement with your heart can transform how people respond to you. Parents of teenagers will generally agree that this phase in their child's life can be a battleground and fraught with hidden dangers and emotional outbursts. My daughter Rose is not the tidiest person on the planet, yet I would constantly nag her 'tidy your room Rose'. I was exhausted from trying to get her to do something she clearly didn't see a need to do – and it took me years to recognise that I needed to just accept that it was her bedroom and up to her if she wanted to live in what I perceived as chaos. I remember sitting down one evening when she told me that she thought we weren't having fun together anymore. I was great when she was ill but apart from that I was always on at her. Boy did those comments hurt me. Rose was right to call me on it. I was either in full-on maternal mode when she was ill or having a go at her about the state of her room. I realised that we were not *connecting* because I was becoming consumed by my work and just played lip service to conversations with her at home. I believe that many people tend to listen with impatience, waiting for the gap so they can make their point. It's easy to listen to the surface words uttered from a colleague, yet without our complete and utter attention we will miss the deeper undercurrents of their communication.

Compelling vision

In the early 1990s I was working with the senior leadership team of a major financial institution who had decided to bring their corporate vision to life with a set of 'behaviours'. I can remember feeling shocked that these behaviours had been developed by the top team then launched to the workforce. One of the behaviours was 'Execute with speed' and generated a hostile reaction. Particularly from employees working in South Africa where gun crime and murder had increased according to key crime trends recorded by the South African police service. A vision is a picture of the future that will create one of three emotional responses. First, if it is uninspiring it will have no impact; second, it can actually stimulate a negative reaction and will 'install' walls; or, thirdly, it can inspire, engage and compel followship. Charismatic people have a clear and compelling vision of what they want to achieve. Charismatic leaders are able to articulate their vision in a way that is inclusive and brings a collective unity towards a common purpose. If each employee can see a compelling vision for their future within the organisation, that vision becomes significant for them personally and stimulates a strong energy of intent, an intensity that others can feel. Charismatic leaders evoke all of the senses as they help to create a powerful visualisation that employees can feel excited about. Martin Luther King's vision for equality and civil rights in the United States was brilliantly conveyed in his 'I have a Dream' speech. The huge scale and confidence he had in his vision is encapsulated in his opening words, 'I am happy to join with you today in what will go down in history as the greatest demonstration for freedom in the history of our nation.' Yet he was able to make this vision relevant for the ordinary person, 'I have a dream that my four little children will one day live in a nation where they will not be judged by the color of their skin but by the content of their character.' In 1966 Richard Schulze, founder of Best Buy, opened his first audio speciality store in Saint Paul, Minnesota. Today this organisation has amassed many prestigious accolades ranging from Best Company of the Year in 2004 by *Forbes* magazine, Speciality Retailer of the Decade to Top 10 of America's Most Generous Corporations. Schulze's vision to solve the unmet needs of customers by relying on employees to determine their needs has been cascaded to every employee in every one of Best Buy's subsidiaries. One of those subsidiaries is Geek Squad who operate as a franchise in Carphone Warehouse retail outlets. Every employee is referred to as an agent and manages their 'precinct' (workstation) wearing an FBI styled uniform. When upgrading my mobile phone recently a Geek Squad agent in Maidstone, England, shared the history of how Geek Squad started and what they stood for. This young man clearly loved his job and was a stunning example of how a global corporation's vision had touched the heart of its front line workforce, even in Kent!

Driving force

The art of motivation is, to put it simply, understanding what is important to each individual. Individuals are motivated by different things, yet these can be generalised into their needs and wants. If their needs aren't satisfied, then the individual will become demotivated. If their needs are satisfied, then what they want becomes their own internal driving force. Every individual is completely unique and consequently has a set of values that are unique to them. These are the fundamental principles and beliefs that are considered worthwhile and desirable by the individual and consequently they hold a lot of emotional intensity. Many leaders make the mistake of trying to motivate employees in the same way or based on what is important to their generalisations of what they believe will motivate others. This approach may work for those employees that have similar values to their leader, yet in the main it will fail. The best way to motivate a person is to identify what they value as important, in context of their career, and then use this information to motivate and leverage their performance. When we experience that the role we perform has purpose and that our work is important and has personal meaning, we trigger a deep motivation that turbocharges our results. Charismatic individuals live their lives based on the criteria of what is important to them. Their values drive and motivate their behaviour, so that they appear and indeed are dynamic, passionate and enthusiastic. You cannot shine or connect to your inner drive and enthusiasm in a career that bores you or a job you dislike.

A compelling vision activates a driving force

Typically, if a person has a clear and compelling vision, motivation naturally follows. If a leader tries to build motivation without utilising the organisation's vision they are in danger of having to 'spoon-feed' and drive motivation. When people are consciously aware of what is important to them in all aspects of their life, they can align their choices to the type of activities that satisfy their innermost emotional needs as well as external hygiene factors. In 2004 I worked in association with Chicago-based Nightingale-Connant on a piece of research with 2,663 organisations. One of the biggest issues identified was when an organisation promoted their top producing salesperson into the role of sales manager. The two roles are so different that the personal career values of the newly promoted sales manager were often no longer satisfied and they would leave. The more an individual understands what motivates them personally, the better equipped they become to build their personal magnetism. When we feel motivated, we are able to tap into the fuel that drives our performance. Motivation gives us reasons to solve problems, overcome difficulties and persevere when the going gets tough. Motivation can transform an ordinary performance into an extraordinary performance because, ultimately, if an individual wants to achieve a particular goal badly enough, they will be prepared to do whatever it takes to get it. Richard Branson was a pretty poor student at school, performing badly in tests and getting low marks and poor grades. This did not stop him from launching his first business at 16, a magazine called *Student*. As a businessman and entrepreneur he is one of the UK's richest people and Virgin is one of the world's most recognised and respected brands. Right now, Richard Branson's vision is for Virgin Galactic to become the world's first space-line and open the space frontier to the general public. He is a charismatic leader with a vision that most leaders would not even think about let alone envision and commit to making it happen.

Energy

The more energy we possess the more positive we feel. According to a study by Lucozade Energy and the Centre for Business Performance at Cranfield School of Management (Schiuma et al., 2006), UK business leaders are losing up to 520 hours of productivity per employee every year because they fail to manage the energy levels of their staff effectively. Additionally they found that nearly 21 million employees regularly lack energy at work, three in four employees are less productive for two hours a day and over 10 million employees strongly agree that their energy levels affects their performance at work. Energy stimulates creativity, successful teamwork and passion. If an individual lacks self-esteem and believes they are not good enough, they start to drain their own energy. If a person has an exciting and compelling vision, this stimulates and increases their energy in themselves as well as others. Each person's driving force will affect the intensity of their energy. I remember when my daughter Rose was looking for her first job. Days of uncertainty began to create a lethargy that sapped every ounce of her energy. She felt continually tired and slept longer hours. When she started her first full-time job her energy levels went through the roof. Almost overnight her passion and motivation gave her a massive energy boost. If we are not tuned into our emotional guidance system our sensory awareness becomes blunted and we fail to pick up upon factors that stimulate or drain our energy. When teams, particularly top teams, are not getting on well together, this has a visible impact on energy levels. Meetings become fraught with either too much emotion (battlegrounds) or complete detachment (graveyards) – both states are extremely draining and as energy levels drop so does the ability to think clearly, positively and quickly. The energy or lack of it generated from the top team will cascade throughout the organisation. The energy generated from an individual or a department who is operating as a silo will find themselves closed to the energy of others because their 'wall' is literally keeping energy out and away from them.

The dance of energy

Charismatic people not only exude high energy levels as you would expect, they are able to tap into the energy of others. The more energy they direct towards others increases the energy they are able to receive and use. Other people amplify the energy of the charismatic person who then amplifies it again as they send it back towards others. Rather than the charismatic individual feeling drained from transmitting so much of their energy they become stimulated and turbocharged from the continual and expanding energy inter-play taking place with others. The balance of an individual's awareness between themselves and others enables a two-way exchange of energy to occur. The more I worked with energy the more I noticed the impact certain factors had on energy levels and how energy levels impacted on so many aspects of a company's general performance. On one end of the spectrum I observed the weakening physiology of downtrodden employees working for a controlling and bullying boss. I noticed how dysfunctional relationships started affecting the physical health of both the employees and the boss. I watched how feedback delivered badly 'knocked the stuffing' out of people on the receiving end of what was fundamentally hurtful criticism. Then at the opposite end of the scale I witnessed the speed that some employees appeared to work at, how their behaviours and actions appeared effortless. I watched people 'open up' when they were genuinely recognised for doing a good job. The complexions of employees became instant 'tells' that informed whether their energy was in balance or was being drained. People with high energy generally look healthier, happier and fitter. Energy is a crucial component for charisma. Understanding it and becoming more sensitive to it is vital to anyone looking to develop their own charismatic presence.

Working below the surface

Charismatic leaders recognise that when they are operating in a state of flow, they are better equipped to enable others to perform in flow. The Charisma Model highlights that restricting your leadership style and approach to what's going on at the surface, fails to create a deep and sustainable change. Working below the surface helps others to understand and appreciate why they are doing what they do. When employees possess more self-awareness they are more likely to perform their roles with their hearts as well as their minds.

Chapter 7

Dowsing for energy

Everyone has the potential to become charismatic. Charisma is a natural state within us all, yet some individuals are able to access this state more easily and more frequently than others. When you feel comfortable, confident and passionate about what you are doing, you radiate an energy that captivates the attention of people around you. The more charisma you access the more your energy grows and expands. In Chapter 2 you learned that your thoughts affect your energy inside and outside your physical body. Your consistent thoughts will become physical manifestations. To put it another way, 'thoughts become things'. If you feel confident and charismatic, the intention of these thoughts will energise more feelings of confidence and charisma. That's why charismatic people have such a potent presence that commands attention with an irresistible magnetic force. It is their energy, their life force that emanates from their thoughts that creates this attraction and attention.

Opening up to energy

Have you ever spent time with someone who has sucked your will to live? Have you entered a room where there were people and had a strong feeling that you could 'cut the atmosphere with a knife'? People often speak about buying their home based on it having 'a nice feel'. Your subtle energy fluctuates all the time, moment by moment. It is continually interacting with the subtle energy of those around us. When you are living in harmony, you can feel it; when you're pushing against the flow, if you have good sensory awareness, you can feel it. Often when people are operating from a survival mechanism, such as high stress levels, they become immune or anaesthetised to feeling what is going on energetically within their bodies. If you have pets or love animals, then you probably know that animals are extremely sensitive and can feel the energy of the earth changing. If there is going to be an earthquake or a thunderstorm or even a heatwave, the animal can feel the energy in the earth build up before it happens, and respond accordingly. Scientific studies have shown that the old wives' tale that cows lie down when it is about to rain may not be so far-fetched after all. Researchers have discovered that cows stand up for longer periods when it is hot and lie down when it is colder. There is a definite link between their behaviour and the weather. If animals naturally possess this level of sensory awareness of the energy from their environment, is it a logical next step to accept that human beings also have this potential capability?

Feeling subtle energies

It is possible to see the subtle energies emanating from an individual and this is often referred to as an aura or our energy body. Unfortunately only a tiny percentage of people can 'see' auras and subtle energies. Children raised by adults who had the belief that they could see auras ensure that their children never lose the belief that it is possible to see subtle energies. This makes learning about energy a challenge in a business context because if it can't be seen or easily 'felt' by the untrained leader it is too vague and abstract to work with on a practical day-to-day basis. So the first step when working with subtle energy is to know how to connect with it. For many people understanding a bit about the theory of energy is not enough to appreciate what factors create such an impact on our energy and how energy causes us to feel. Because subtle energy is exactly that – subtle – it is intangible and, for most people, cannot be seen. This prompted me to explore ways that would show anyone how to access information relating to their energy. I wanted to help leaders tune into their body's natural energetic highs and lows. This ability to connect with and work with energy is just another way of developing sensory awareness and emotional intelligence. Working with energy requires you to use and trust your unconscious mind. The beliefs and values from your unconscious mind are not restricted by the same logical filters used by your conscious mind. The prime directive from your unconscious mind is to protect you and keep you safe. When you work with your unconscious mind and begin to listen to your intuition you may feel that you are making things up. Your unconscious mind works quickly. It may show you a picture, send you a seemingly 'random' thought or even give you a physical feeling within your body. As your confidence and trust in your unconscious mind grows, you'll find it easier to hear and communicate with it. Imagine a door that connects your conscious and unconscious mind. To open the door to your unconscious mind, simply take a deep breath in through your nose and exhale out through your mouth and relax. Then, focus on a single point in front of you and expand your awareness into your periphery. Allow your lower jaw muscles to relax and after a few seconds you may notice that you feel a little tranced out and light-headed – you have just opened the door to your unconscious mind.

Every moment, your energy changes and these changes can be felt inside or outside your body. Rub your hands together quickly, then let them go, keeping them nearly touching, and feel the 'magnetic pull' between your hands. Sometimes you may become aware that parts of your body feel warm and other parts feel cold. Normally, high amounts of positive energy feel warm and tingly. Energy that is negative that is close to the surface (think of an eruption of anger) can also feel warm. Negative energy or blockages feel cold. Don't believe me? Try this exercise. Think about an event in your life that still causes you to feel upset. As you think about this moment, notice the feelings within your body. Where are you feeling them? How do they feel? Most people describe this feeling as draining, hard or cold. Now, think about someone you really love and imagine they are sitting in front of you. Notice that look of real love in their eyes and allow yourself to hear the sound of their voice as the love you feel for them grows and expands within you. Whereabouts in your body are you feeling this sensation of love? How does it feel? Most people will describe this feeling as warm and tingly.

Measuring energy

When I first started delivering my charisma seminars at Shakespeare's Globe Theatre in 2008 I wanted to include a process that would measure the energy of attendees before and after my two-day seminar. I used Kirlian photography – a photographic process invented by Semyon Davidovich Kirlian in 1939. This process captures the electromagnetic field around the objects being photographed. Later research by Alexander Gurwitsch showed that a Kirlian photograph could indicate levels and issues relating to physical and emotional health. The principle behind Kirlian photography is based on the knowledge that an individual's thoughts, emotions and movements produce a tiny electrical charge. According to the basic law of physics, every electrical charge produces a corresponding electromagnetic field that can provide meaningful information about that person. Due to the abundance of nerve endings in the hands and the fact that hands are easy and practical to photograph, they are used to produce an image of an individual's electromagnetic field. German scientist Peter Mandel devoted 15 years to photographing and interpreting over 800,000 Kirlian photos to identify emotional and physical issues. According to neuroscience, the left and more logical brain hemisphere operates the right side of the body. The right hemisphere of the brain is more intuitive, creative and emotional. This operates the left side of the body. In terms of my definition of charisma – *an authentic power that captivates the hearts and minds of others* – the right hand when photographed indicates the relative dominance (or not) of the logical mind compared to the left hand that is more heart centred. Consequently, a Kirlian photograph would immediately show a leader's preference or balance between their heart and mind. When I studied Mandel's analysis system further I saw that there were similarities between his interpretation around the dominance of each finger and my own five attributes that formed the Symbol of Star Quality. It wasn't a perfect fit yet there were striking similarities.

Digits	Related attribute from Symbol of Star Quality	Mandel's digit assessment
Little finger	Energy flow within the individual	Spiritual potential/expression
Ring finger	Sensory awareness and emotional connection	Creative potential/expression
Middle finger	Driving force and career values	Career satisfaction/ability
Index finger	Compelling vision that encourages followship	Leadership potential/authority expression
Thumb	Self-esteem, authenticity, being grounded	Action/resoluteness

Was it possible that a Kirlian photograph of a pair of hands could indicate areas within my own Symbol of Star Quality model that were impeding the flow of that person's charisma?

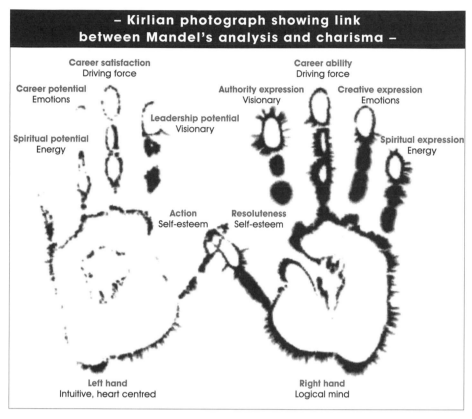

– Kirlian photograph showing link between Mandel's analysis and charisma –

Career satisfaction
Driving force

Career ability
Driving force

Career potential
Emotions

Authority expression
Visionary

Creative expression
Emotions

Leadership potential
Visionary

Spiritual potential
Energy

Spiritual expression
Energy

Action
Self-esteem

Resoluteness
Self-esteem

Left hand
Intuitive, heart centred

Right hand
Logical mind

Handing out electric shock treatment

Imagine you are a delegate arriving for one of my seminars held in the somewhat unusual environment of Shakespeare's Globe Theatre. An expert in Kirlian photography would grab you, before you had even grabbed a cup of coffee and ask you to take off your shoes. You would then be escorted into a pitch black tent and your hands would be placed onto a sheet of photographic film that was laid out on top of a metal plate. A high voltage current would be given to create the initial exposure. Yes, in those days we really did give attendees an electric shock before the seminar had even started! When developed your Kirlian photograph would show a glowing silhouette of light around your hands. Our Kirlian expert would then analyse this photograph and give you insights into your emotional and physical states. We repeated this process again at the end of the seminar so that attendees received a visible record of how their energy had changed by the end of their two days with us. After two years of using this process, 98 per cent of attendees had a stronger, bigger silhouette in their second photograph. Although the process was interesting, I stopped using it in 2010 because unsurprisingly it unsettled attendees at the start of the seminar and it was difficult to assess whether I had inadvertently lowered their energy by inducing anxiety with the dark tent and electric shock. I also felt that I was dabbling in the realms of pseudoscience and, ultimately, it didn't feel right. What Kirlian photography did achieve was that it convinced me of the presence of an electromagnetic field, an aura or an energy body that is inherent in every living thing. I intuitively knew that charismatic individuals possessed large auras so I began searching for another way of identifying how I could help others to develop their own energy levels. Inspiration appears in many guises and on a sunny summer's afternoon I had invited a number of my mother's friends to my home to celebrate her 70th birthday. One of these was a lady I have known since I was 30 – Sue Skinner. She had phoned to ask for my permission to dowse my house. I was intensely curious and agreed. She turned up with a pair of L-shaped metal rods and began walking around my house telling me where there was good and negative energy. This introduction to dowsing started my fascinating journey into the unseen world.

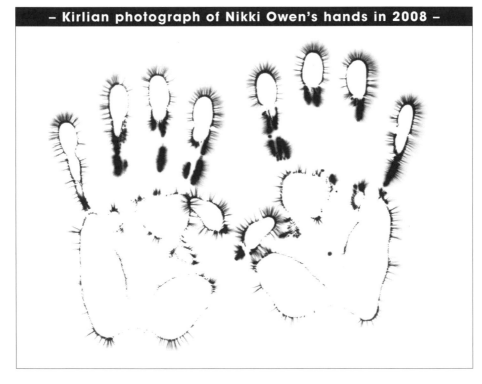
– Kirlian photograph of Nikki Owen's hands in 2008 –

Seeing the unseen

Dowsing is the ability to search for that which is otherwise hidden from view. It can be used to find water, pinpoint gas leaks, find oil and obtain information about our bodies that is not consciously known to us. Dowsing demonstrates the existence of the invisible world of subtle energy. Quantum physicists believe that everything is created from energy and energy has a vibration. This means that everything and everyone has their own vibrational frequency. In a dowsing context you are tuning your awareness into the vibrational frequency of what you want to connect with. You employ your unconscious mind and give a command or ask a question. For example, 'Show me the edge of this person's aura.' An electrical impulse is then sent to your brain and, in response, a compatible wavelength is created and another electrical impulse is sent back. These impulses create a micro-constriction of muscles, which push energy down along your arm to reach your dowsing 'tool'. Since 'positive' or 'negative' emotional states are represented by different energetic vibrations this creates different movements in the dowser's tools. Dowsing tools take many different forms ranging from old-fashioned hazel sticks to rods, pendulums and bobbers. Whilst the dowser holds a dowsing tool, the actual dowsing instrument is the human body. The mind is the receiver or antenna and the dowsing tool simply amplifies that signal. In reality, the unconscious mind is constantly picking up millions of environmental signals every second, of which the conscious mind is unaware. When dowsing you are unconsciously and involuntarily moving the dowsing tool.

Who uses dowsing?

Many types of industries employ the services of professional dowsers. Utilities companies teach their engineers how to dowse so they can pinpoint gas leaks. Building surveyors use dowsers to map out the location of underground pipes, tunnels and mineshafts before determining whether a plot of land is suitable for building and construction. The FBI use dowsing to find missing people and another high profile case was when, during the Falklands War, the British Army taught their troops how to dowse for bombs in the ground. Dowsing is used to locate water lying in underground streams, in prospecting for minerals and oil, soil testing for acidity, and in archaeological searches. Despite the many credible industries that depend on the findings of a dowser, there are an equal number of sceptics that try to disprove the insights gained from dowsing. Albert Einstein was convinced of the authenticity of dowsing. He said (*Living*, 2008),

> I know very well that many scientists consider dowsing as they do astrology, as a type of ancient superstition. According to my conviction this is, however, unjustified. The dowsing rod is a simple instrument which shows the reaction of the human nervous system to certain factors which are unknown to us at this time.

If Einstein believed in it, then I was prepared to experiment with it myself. I joined The British Society of Dowsers and started to explore this controversial subject. Using a set of simple L-shaped metal dowsing rods I embarked upon a quest to find out whether there was such a thing as an average aura size and what factors impacted either positively or negatively on the size of an aura. Having experimented at home with my friends and family I decided to teach attendees at my seminars how to dowse for the size of people's auras. Everyone has the ability to dowse and everyone has the potential to block it. When dowsing you are operating with your unconscious mind rather than your conscious mind and the differences in the size of people's auras can only be clearly assessed if the individual who is having their aura measured is able to access different emotional states. Thinking about love does not necessarily mean that you are feeling love. Talking about anger does not necessarily mean that you are feeling angry.

– EXERCISE: HOW TO DOWSE USING DOWSING RODS –

The ideal state of mind for dowsing is relaxed and open so you can tune into a high level of self-awareness. You measure what you focus on. So if you want to look for water, you focus on water, if you want to measure the size of a person's aura you focus on that person and hold your rods in front of you as if you are impersonating a Dalek. Everyone's dowsing rods move in a way that is right for them. For some people their rods open at the edge of an aura, for others, their rods close. Sometimes if a person's conscious mind is blocking the process, that person may only experience a tiny twitch of movement in their rods. The structure of the command or question used in dowsing is absolutely vital. If you want to measure John Smith's aura, this is too general; far better to say 'Show me the edge of John Smith's aura' as you walk backwards very slowly.

Factors that affect energy

I use dowsing to highlight and demonstrate what happens energetically when an individual is operating in 'survival' mode and when they are operating in 'growth' mode. The average person's aura will typically treble in size when they are operating in growth in comparison to operating in survival. This is pretty amazing given that people are simply *recalling* a time in their past when they were operating in survival. This shows you how potent your memories are when it comes to their impact on your emotions and consequently your energy field. During the five years I devoted to testing my methods, I was able to draw the following conclusions:

- A healthy person's aura is about 1.8 metres, which extends all around them as if the person is inside an egg of energy.
- Criticism shrinks the other person's aura as well as the aura of the person delivering the criticism.
- The average person can increase their aura range to 10 metres when they access feelings of love and gratitude.
- Mobile phones generally reduce the size of a person's aura – this is why I always recommend that people don't sleep with their phone on their bedside table.
- Insincere praise will reduce the other person's aura whilst genuine heartfelt praise/compliments/feedback treble both people's auras.
- Negative self-talk shrinks a person's aura whilst positive self-talk increases their aura.
- People respond very differently to change. Using a task where individuals were asked to stand on a balance board to simulate

uncertainty, most people's aura initially reduced, yet there was a huge variance with the speed with which auras started to expand. Some people's auras were stimulated and excited by the uncertainty/change whilst other people's auras diminished to an extent where they could no longer balance on their board.

- People's auras would dramatically reduce when they a) thought about a person they disliked and b) thought about a task they disliked.
- Everyone was able to protect their aura size from 'energy vampires' or people that drained them simply by *imagining* they were inside a translucent bubble.
- When people are in rapport they collectively create a threefold increase in the size of both auras, demonstrating the real impact of engagement and collaboration.
- If one person is accessing negative thoughts and the other person is accessing positive thoughts, a third person coming into contact with these two people at the same time will have their aura reduced. This helps to explain why disengagement is so infectious. According to an article 'The high cost of disengaged employees' from Gallup Business Journal 'actively disengaged people... believe that they're doing what needs to [be] done, and everyone else is wrong. Negativity is like a blood clot, and actively disengaged employees sometimes clot together in groups that support and reinforce their beliefs' (2002).
- During discussions, if one person dominated the discussion their aura would increase at the expense of other people present at the discussion. It was as if one dominant person was 'stealing' the energy from other members of the group. The other people's auras reduced significantly.

Measuring well-being

Every year the British Society of Dowsers holds a conference, usually at the Royal Agricultural College in Cirencester, and in 2010 I was lucky enough to meet one of the speakers, Elizabeth Brown, a dowser with over 20 years' experience. Elizabeth's groundbreaking work in the field of dowsing to identify a causative diagnosis for major physical and emotional illnesses has transformed many lives. Inspired by Elizabeth's techniques I started applying dowsing to measure three chemicals released from the brain during one-to-one sessions with my clients.

- Serotonin – acts as a neurotransmitter, a type of chemical that helps relay signals from one area of the brain to another. Although serotonin is manufactured in the brain, where it performs its primary functions, some 90 per cent of our serotonin supply is found in the digestive tract and in blood platelets. Because of the widespread distribution of its cells, it influences a variety of psychological and other body functions. Of the approximately 40 million brain cells, most are influenced either directly or indirectly by serotonin. I knew that low serotonin usually indicated a depressed state and thought that this would be a great way for me to measure an individual's general well-being before and after their session.

- Oxytocin – often referred to as the 'trust and empathy hormone'. New research is suggesting that oxytocin plays a crucial part in enabling us to not just forge and strengthen our social relations, but in helping us to stave off a number of psychological and physiological problems as well. Given its ability to break down social barriers, induce feelings of optimism, increase self-esteem and build trust, oxytocin is increasingly being seen as something that can help people overcome their social inhibitions and fears. Because self-esteem is one of my five pillars for creating charisma, I am able to get a general impression about the individual's self-worth based on what percentage of oxytocin is present in their body.

- Cortisol – produced in the adrenal cortex and plays an important role in regulating blood sugar, energy production, inflammation, the immune system and healing. Cortisol is elevated in response to stress and puts the body on red alert. As the body responds to cumulative stress, it eventually moves into a phase of exhaustion that depletes the body's reserves of nutritional elements and resilience. If an individual's cortisol is high then it indicates the presence of stress and anxiety and shows me that at a cellular level they are operating in survival mode.

Dowsing for energy increases sensory awareness

As more organisations embrace the value of increasing the emotional intelligence of their leadership team, I observed during my seminars and masterclasses that as leaders started to learn how to dowse they became more emotionally receptive, sensitive and intuitive. Dowsing was a great way to accelerate their sensory awareness. During masterclass sessions with CEO groups I often witness a 'softening' of these logical and matter-of-fact business men and women as they become more connected with their emotions during the dowsing exercises. This is because the only way to dowse effectively is to switch off the conscious mind and trust the unconscious mind. This stimulates a light trance-like state that sharpens people's awareness of their senses. Most people introduced to dowsing react with initial scepticism until they experience the way it works. Having now introduced thousands of business leaders to the thought-provoking world of dowsing, I have encountered one extreme negative reaction. I was delivering a charisma masterclass for a group of business leaders on the outskirts of Dublin. Many of them were staunch Catholics and saw me and dowsing as – and I quote verbatim – 'the spawn of the devil'. I was genuinely stunned by this reaction and upon further questioning I realised that when I was asking, 'Show me the edge of this person's aura', my audience were unclear as to whom I was addressing. Nowadays I am very quick to point out that you are asking *your unconscious mind* this question.

– EXERCISE: HOW TO DOWSE WITH YOUR BODY –

Sometimes in life we may be faced with having to make a difficult decision, or we may be presented with an array of options. Stand for a moment and pull up your posture so that you feel as if an invisible cord is pulling up the top of your head. Keep your knees slightly soft and have your feet shoulder width apart. Allow your arms to remain relaxed by the side of your body. Close your eyes for a moment and just notice that your body starts to sway a little bit, forwards and backwards. Ask yourself a closed question that requires a 'yes' or 'no' response. Ask a question that prompts a 'yes' response. Notice whether your body sways forwards or backwards. Ask yourself another closed question that prompts a 'no' answer and notice the direction your body sways towards. This process enables you to make a decision that's fully aligned with your core self.

Chapter 8

Getting energy to flow

Emotions are a great feedback mechanism that indicates whether we are vibrating at a frequency that supports our performance or sabotages it. To appreciate the difference between 'good vibes' and 'bad vibes', imagine dropping two rocks of the same size, from the same height, into a pond at the same time. At the point that the ripples made by each rock converge, the power of the 'entangled' energy waves is amplified, and the height of the combined waves is greater than the heights of the individual ripples that gave rise to them. This phenomenon, explaining the science behind 'good vibes', is known as *constructive interference*. If these same rocks are dropped out of sync, they will create ripples/energy waves that are not in harmony. This energy will not amplify the power of the out-of-phase waves. It will in fact dissipate it. This phenomenon of cancelling energy is called *destructive interference*, and it describes the energetic effect of 'bad vibes'. This explains disengagement from an energetic perspective. The impact a leader has on their team's vibes has an effect far more dramatic than we realise. When we 'entangle' with someone else's energy, we want the interference to be constructive because it doubles the collective energy (good vibes) not destructive, which drains the collective energy (bad vibes). We want colleague interactions to increase our energy, as well as theirs, not deplete it. Constructive interference creates high performance, harmonious teams, creative thinking and a collaborative environment where employees are more likely to operate from a growth mindset. That's why living and working in a harmonious and collaborative environment is *scientifically proven* to be so much better for us all. When we access our natural state of charisma we enable our energy to *constructively interfere* with others.

The Love Study

This ability to develop strong connections with others has been explored in a scientific experiment known as 'The Love Study' by Elisabeth Targ, a mainstream psychiatrist, and Marilyn Schlitz, vice president for research and education at the Institute of Noetic Sciences (Institute of Noetic Sciences, n.d.). The Love Study was the first scientific demonstration of exactly how intention physically affects its recipient. The Love Study, so-called because it was partially funded by the Institute for Research on

Unlimited Love, measured what would happen in the nervous system of one person when exposed to strong intentions from another person at a distance. This laboratory study recruited long-term, loving couples as participants, and trained the healthy partner (the other partner had cancer) in compassionate intention – directing selfless love to another – and explored whether training and practice in sending intentions would have any measurable effects. This experiment showed that when individuals had established a visual connection (staring at an individual was classified as a connection), the electrical signalling in the brains of both 'connected' people becomes synchronised. The frequencies, amplitudes and phrases of their brain waves start operating in tandem. In physics, this is referred to as entrainment, which means that two oscillating systems fall into synchronicity. This phenomenon explains why being present with people builds deeper relationships. Energy flows where your attention goes, so if your attention is wondering to what you are going to have for tea, then you are energising your thoughts rather than energising your relationship interaction. Bill Clinton, former US president, is exceptionally good at connecting with people. His awareness and presence causes people to feel a strong bond and his energy can be felt from across a crowded room. High energy levels create a feel-good feeling within us, we perform better, we are healthier and happier. Low energy levels creates dysfunction within our system and also impacts on the energy of others. Charismatic leaders unconsciously utilise their energy to appeal to employees by exuding high energy levels that connect with and stimulate the flow of energy in others – and this feels wonderful. Essentially a charismatic leader, albeit often unwittingly, establishes a conditioned response from their followers who make the neurological and often unconscious link, 'charismatic leader = feeling fabulous'.

Energy interplays

When relationships are collaborative and constructive the flow of energy is equally shared between both people. When we experience conflict in a relationship we unconsciously try to *control the behaviour and energy* of the other person. The way we do this is by employing a 'control drama'. When another person evokes a strong negative response within you, it signals that there is an imbalance or blockage in the energy flow of both of you. This is one of the reasons why relationships accelerate our ability to grow and develop because they trigger 'our stuff'. Learning how to create energetic balance and flow within relationships is incredibly helpful not only for building our charisma but for our own personal development.

– Energy interplays –

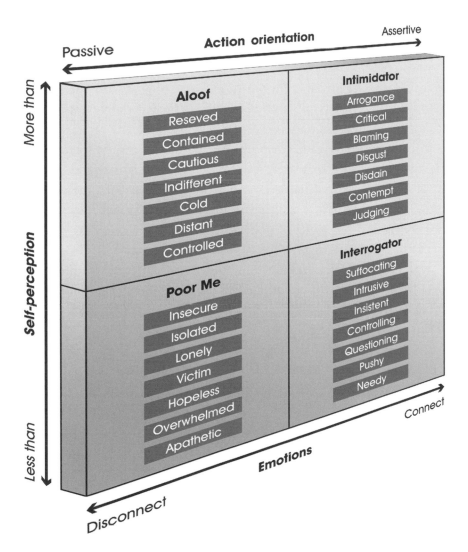

Control dramas

In James Redfield's (1994) book, *The Celestine Prophecy*, he introduces four different control dramas that inspired me to understand more about how people unconsciously seek to control energy by playing out their different 'dramas'. At the core of this model is the presupposition that when relationships are out of balance, they drain our energy (destructive interference). The more dysfunctional the relationship the more energy we lose from our system and we feel tired, depressed and negative. Because the unconscious mind's prime directive is to protect us, we unconsciously seek to 'steal' energy from the other person by taking control of their energy. Some people do this by playing the drama of 'poor me', where they act out the role of victim and become insecure, vulnerable and apathetic. The perception of self is that they are not as good as everyone else, not as lucky, not as clever, and they disconnect emotionally from the other person as their focus turns inwards and everything becomes 'all about me'. I have a friend I have known for a long time who has been through years of hardship because of becoming involved with strong, controlling and abusive men. She is one of life's victims and has not yet understood that she is choosing to stay in these damaging relationships because she gains energy from being the victim. Some people seek to control the other person by playing the drama of 'intimidator', finding that blaming and judging others enables them to assert their power as they seem to crave even more emotional connection to feed their energy cravings. In my early 20s I lived with a man who was judgemental and controlling – he seemed to enjoy my fear. The longer I stayed in the relationship the more frightening he appeared and I slipped into a deep depression – it felt as if he was draining me of every ounce of energy. Other people withdraw 'into their cave' and play the drama of 'aloof', disconnecting completely from the other person and the situation. They appear cold, distant, controlled and indifferent, and have a tendency to look down on others. As my beautiful daughter Rose became a teenager she started to distance herself from me as I was not a cool person to hang out with anymore. I initially struggled with this reserved aspect of her personality without recognising that it was an important part of becoming a teenager. The final drama is 'interrogator', who has an insatiable need to connect and know everything. They can be suffocating, intrusive, insistent and needy and are driven by feelings of inadequacy in these moments. I played this drama all the time with Rose – I must have driven her mad – 'Have you done your homework?' 'Where will you be tonight?' 'What are you planning to do with the rest of your life?'… Thank goodness Rose and I have evolved through this challenging time in our relationship!

Observing your control drama

Having understood James Redfield's control dramas I knew that if people simply gave their energy away, others would feel energised, yet after a time the individual would feel completely exhausted and washed out. Equally, if people become too inwardly focused, too self-absorbed they drain the energy from those around them. I decided to develop Redfield's concept into a practical business model that blended the need to connect with others with levels of passive/assertive energy and how this combination was demonstrated through specific behaviours. Simply by starting to pay attention to control dramas enables you to detach momentarily from relationships as you observe the 'dramas' being used. The shift in your awareness creates a shift in the energetic interplay and the locus of energetic control shifts accordingly. I will often name the drama as it is being played out and seek to uncover what the other person really wants from me. This level of direct honesty interrupts the energetic pattern and consequently shakes up the energy. For example, 'Your behaviour is very aloof, I feel you are withdrawing emotionally. Do you want me to leave you alone?' (aloof); 'You are talking as if you are in a hopeless situation and there is nothing you can do to change it. Is this really how you feel?' (poor me); 'I'm finding your actions/words intimidating. How do you really want me to feel?' (intimidator); 'Your questions feel very intrusive and I can feel myself putting up a wall. What do you really want to know?' (interrogator).

I have noticed how easily people slip into their control dramas with certain people. In marriages, relationships between parents and their teenage children, manager and employee. After a while the relationship is the 'trigger' for the energetic interplay and it evolves into an ingrained negative pattern. This is why recognising and naming the drama can be vital when 'interrupting' this draining and destructive process.

Energy flow and awareness

Charismatic leaders possess huge reservoirs of energy. How do they do it and where do they get their energy from? First, they balance their awareness between their self and others. A tiny shift in a person's awareness has a big impact on the flow of their energy. If your own awareness is exclusively focused on you then you are flowing subtle energy to yourself. Unfortunately, when working with others your dominating awareness of yourself will drain energy from other people. This is why when one person dominates a meeting the other people feel drained and bored. Alternatively, if all your awareness is on the other person and you continually seek to please and help others, you will energise others whilst draining your own energy levels. This is why a tendency to give to others at the cost of yourself is very detrimental to your emotional health. There will come a point when one day you are simply too exhausted to help anyone including yourself. When you are able to balance your awareness between yourself and others you are simultaneously sending and receiving energy. When you place yourself as equally as important as others you are able to transmit more energy because you are receiving more energy.

The chakras

As my understanding of subtle energy increased I was introduced to the concept of chakras. In layman's terms these energy centres are a bit like doorways located throughout the body where subtle energy flows in and out. According to ancient wisdom, the chakras are energy vortices or spirals that exist within the human subtle energy field known as our etheric body. Each vortex is a swirling mass that draws energy into its centre and moves it out as it transmits life force energy to and around the body. The word chakra comes from the Sanskrit and means 'wheel'. There are seven major chakras as well as other minor chakras. These swirling subtle energy centres are situated along the spinal column and are located between the base of the spine and the crown of the head. Primitive people knew when they felt out of balance because they intuitively felt a shift in their energy linked to a certain part of their body. Information on chakras found in ancient texts has been substantiated by growing numbers of western academics and cognitive scientists who are now endorsing eastern philosophy, particularly around meditation and chakras.

Impact of blocked chakras on well-being

The seven major chakras are linked with each other and connected to parts of our cellular structure so we can receive, absorb and send life energies. They are located around the major nerve ganglia and link with the glands of the endocrine system. The chakras vibrate at different frequencies as they transmit energy. Each is associated with a vibrational frequency, a characteristic colour, a sense organ and an endocrine gland. Chakras create vortices drawing life experiences into them. When we are overworked, tired, generally stressed and feeling out of balance, then these negative emotions can become stuck causing blockages in the chakras. The root or first chakra rotates at the slowest speed; the crown or seventh chakra at the highest speed. According to eastern traditions, each chakra is stimulated by its own colour. The chakra colours are red, orange, yellow, green, blue, indigo and violet. The size and brightness of the chakras vary from individual to individual and are affected by personal and physical development, physical conditions, energy levels, disease and stress. If your chakras are not balanced, or if your chakras are blocked, you can feel that your basic life force has slowed down. You may feel listless, tired, out of sorts or depressed. Physical bodily functions become affected, making you more prone to illness and disease. When your chakras are out of balance, your thought processes and emotional state are affected, leading to a negative outlook on life in general. If your chakras are too open, it can cause emotional overload, with too much energy going through your body. When your chakras are functioning normally, each will be open and spinning at the right speed to enable the flow of energy into and out of your body. You will feel emotionally stable, healthy and alert.

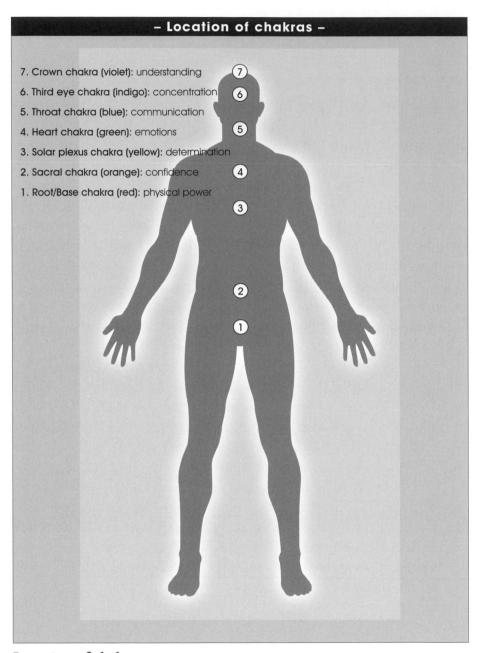

7. Crown chakra (violet): understanding

6. Third eye chakra (indigo): concentration

5. Throat chakra (blue): communication

4. Heart chakra (green): emotions

3. Solar plexus chakra (yellow): determination

2. Sacral chakra (orange): confidence

1. Root/Base chakra (red): physical power

Location of chakras

When working with your chakras it helps to know a little bit about where they are located, each chakra's core function and the specific effects you may experience if they are out of balance. Sometimes your chakras may be overactive or underactive.

1. Root/Base chakra – associated with the colour red and located between your anus and genitalia. This chakra is about physical power and your connection with the earth. When you feel grounded you are able to deal with negative emotions more effectively. If this chakra is overactive then you are likely to experience an obsession with money and possessions. You may be prone to angry outbursts and others may view you as egotistical and controlling. If this chakra is underactive then you may feel weak, vulnerable, lacking in confidence and with a fear of abandonment. Physical illnesses associated with the root chakra include sexual dysfunction, tiredness and depression, and issues with the prostrate, reproductive systems and the bladder. When your root chakra is in balance you're likely to feel healthy and secure. Others will view you as authentic, kind and genuine.

2. Sacral chakra – associated with the colour orange and located just below your belly button. This chakra is about confidence, your self-worth and your creativity. The sacral chakra is affected by the ease with which you relate and connect to others. If this chakra is overactive, then you'll experience aggression, a reluctance around being alone, being overeager in relationships and obsessed with sex. Others may describe you as very driven, ambitious and manipulative. If this chakra is underactive, then you'll feel overly sensitive, shy, timid and guilty about sex. Physical illnesses associated with the sacral chakra include kidney problems, constipation, impotence, menstrual disorders, pancreas issues and diabetes. When this chakra is balanced you'll feel more creative, sociable, intuitive and attuned to your own feelings. You'll experience a sense of belonging and feel optimistic about life.

3. Solar plexus chakra – associated with the colour yellow and located at the top of your ribcage just below your sternum. If this chakra is overactive, then others will perceive you as a demanding, judgemental worrier. You'll continually set high standards in a quest for perfection. Sometimes you will be too much 'in your head' rather than connecting emotionally. If this chakra is underactive you're likely to feel depressed, confused, worried and these emotions will drain your confidence. You may feel insecure, needing constant reassurance and be overly concerned with what others think of you. Physical illnesses associated with this chakra are centred mainly around digestive disorders, and

physical and mental exhaustion. When this chakra is balanced you'll feel empowered, strong, brave and confident.

4. Heart chakra – associated with the colour green and located in the middle of your chest. When this chakra is overactive you may experience a 'martyr' attitude and be possessive and moody. You may feel out of control emotionally and demand much from others. When this chakra is underactive you'll feel repressed, indecisive, scared about letting go of relationships, getting hurt or being abandoned. You may feel unworthy of love and feel panic around the idea of being rejected. Physical issues associated with the heart chakra include heart and circulation problems, high blood pressure, asthma, tension, inability to sleep well and a weakened immune system. When this chakra is in balance you'll feel unconditional love and a deep connection with nature and your spiritual purpose. You'll be better able to deal with loss, hardships, rejection and bereavement.

5. Throat chakra – associated with the colour blue and located in your throat just in front of your Adam's apple if you're male and in the middle of your throat if you're female. When this chakra is overactive you'll notice that you talk excessively and have an inability to listen to others. You'll feel afraid of silences and others may describe you as being permanently on 'transmit'. If this chakra is underactive you may stutter and have a real fear of speaking. You may be scared about being judged or rejected. Physical issues relating to this chakra include thyroid imbalances, general throat problems, and neck and jaw problems. When this chakra is balanced you'll feel able to speak easily from your heart and will be able to listen beyond the words of others as well as to your own 'inner voice'.

6. Third eye chakra – associated with the colour indigo and located in your forehead just above the centre of where your eyebrows would meet. If this chakra is overactive, then you rely more on science, your intellect and what you are able to tangibly see on the surface. When the third eye chakra is underactive, then you'll feel afraid or sceptical about trusting your intuition. You may experience a poor memory and have difficulty concentrating. Physical issues associated with this chakra include any problems in the brain, headaches, neurological disorders, mental disorders and learning disabilities. When the third

eye chakra is balanced you'll experience high levels of emotional intelligence, a vivid imagination and a connection to the universe.

7. Crown chakra – associated with the colour violet and located at the top of your head. When this chakra is overactive you may experience a need to overthink and overanalyse your experiences. When this chakra is underactive then you may experience anxiety, confusion and a general sense of 'brain fog'. Physical illnesses associated with the crown chakra include genetic disorders, bone problems, paralysis and disorders of the nervous system. When balanced you'll feel a deep sense of wisdom and a sense that you are working in a state of flow. You'll feel more spiritually awakened and trust your intuition.

Balancing chakras

My opportunity to experiment with chakras was presented when Reiki Master Sue Skinner, who has tirelessly championed and mentored my work on charisma since 2007, popped over for Sunday lunch. I must have looked a bit tired because she offered to 'balance my chakras'. As Sue started working on me I felt gentle fluttering movements inside my body and became deeply relaxed. Every now and then I felt a bit nauseous and emotional yet it was a wonderfully calming experience. My energy felt totally different. Your chakras may be out of balance because you have unreleased emotional issues that are blocking the performance of some or all of your chakras or you may have insufficient levels of positive emotions within your body.

Bringing chakra balancing into business

I immediately started to introduce this process into my masterclasses and seminars. Showing business leaders how to balance the chakras of others was quite a nerve wracking experience – had I gone too far? Amazingly this chakra balancing session proved to be a massive hit for over 90 per cent of attendees and most of them were able to do it. My process was based on the principle that buried negative emotions will clog up the chakras causing them to slow down or stop working effectively. If these doorways to the energy system remains closed or stuck, imagine how quickly an energetic imbalance will be created. I found that using a pendulum works really well with business people because it shows them the direction and rotation speed of their 'invisible' chakras. This process is customised to each person's energetic requirements. Some people need a lot of negative energy removed whilst others need to receive more positive energy.

What to expect during a chakra balance

I have been using chakra balancing in a corporate setting since 2011 and have gathered feedback based on what attendees typically feel during this process. Generally they feel extremely relaxed and find it easy to drift into a light sleep. Fluttering feelings and sensations of warmth are frequently experienced and many people see bright colours. Some people feel emotional and most people experience a sharpening up of their sensory awareness. I recommend that people try to balance their chakras at least once every couple of months to help minimise stress and ensure optimum health and well-being. I have included my process to balance your own chakras at the end of this book. You can also access a video demonstration located on my website nikkijowen.com/howtobalancechakras

The Energy Compass

When you combine the dual components of balanced awareness (between self and others) with balanced chakras you create the right platform energetically for charisma to grow and develop. I call this platform the Energy Compass. If you feel you have an energetic imbalance this platform can be helpful in terms of identifying the cause of the imbalance and help you get your energy back into flow again. The ability to send and receive energy simultaneously ensures you are able to operate with high energy for longer periods.

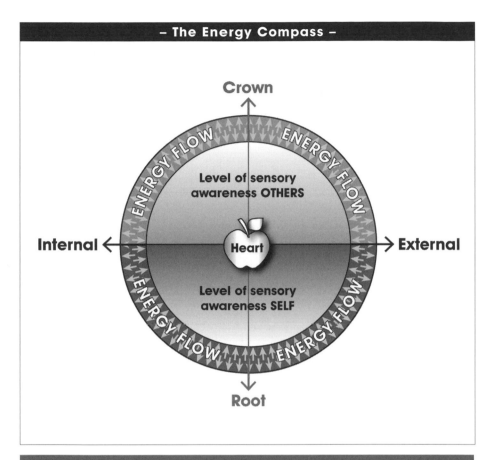

– The Energy Compass –

Crown

ENERGY FLOW

ENERGY FLOW

Level of sensory awareness OTHERS

Internal ← Heart → External

Level of sensory awareness SELF

ENERGY FLOW

ENERGY FLOW

Root

– CHARISMA ENHANCER: BREATHE WELL –

Incorrect breathing reduces your body's ability to deliver oxygen into your cells and will create a survival operating response. Your brain uses 20 per cent of the oxygen you inhale. Your heart uses huge amounts of oxygen to ensure it keeps beating around 100,000 beats each day. If your muscles are not oxygenated well then they become stiff, tense and tired. When you breathe correctly your energy increases, you feel calm, harmonious and happier. Your cellular body operates in growth and your natural authentic charisma flows with greater ease. By devoting a minimum of ten minutes each day to mindful breathing you'll notice a significant increase in your sensory awareness.

1. Breathe in through your nose because your nose filters and refines the incoming air and helps to protect your lungs from air that is raw, cold, dry and full of viruses and bacteria.

2. Breathe with your diaphragm because it takes away the pressure from your heart and supports your lymphatic system, which will boost your body's immune system. This means you are expanding your belly. If you find this uncomfortable initially, lie on your back and place a book on your stomach. Aim to lift the book every time you inhale.

3. Extend your exhalation, which increases relaxation and makes your inhale deeper and more rhythmical. Your belly should be drawn back towards the spine. Ideally breathe in for about three seconds and exhale for five seconds.

4. Pay attention to your posture to ensure you are sitting or standing up straight. This gives your diaphragm space to work more effectively.

5. Focus your attention on your breathing so that you can improve the form of each breath and this clears your mind of your 'monkey chatter'.

Once you feel comfortable and relaxed, close your eyes and use your imagination to visualise breathing in different colours. Notice whether you feel any subtle changes between colours.

Breathing correctly is one of the quickest ways to improve your sensory awareness because you are more relaxed and therefore more tuned in to the messages being communicated from your unconscious mind.

Chapter 9

One bad apple

Charismatic leaders inspire others to want to follow them. They articulate and convey their vision in a way that compels others to want to engage with their vision. So what is happening underneath the surface of a charismatic leader that enables them to effortlessly attract others towards their vision? One of the most exciting experiments I ran with attendees at the Globe involved one person holding their dowsing rods with their eyes closed. Their partner would decide silently whether they were going to use the power of their thoughts to either open or close the other person's rods. It was eerily spooky watching this silent process as people's rods started to move in the direction determined by their partner's thoughts. We were averaging around a 65 per cent success rate. This caused me to reflect on the question: if a pair of dowsing rods can be moved as a result of another person's thoughts, then can the energy of our focused intent actually have the power to affect reality?

Focused intent

Danish physicist Niels Bohr and his German protégé Werner Heisenberg, who were quantum physics pioneers, realised that the structure of the atoms that make up our universe are not little solar systems of billiard balls but a tiny cloud of probability. Our reality resembles unset jelly – it is fluid and open to influence. Molecules exist in a state of pure potential and will only become 'real and set' once observed. At the quantum level, packets of pulsating energy interact with each other continuously and are invisibly connected by a giant web. If something happens on one part of the web it will send reverberations through other parts of the web so, in effect, any 'event' at a quantum level can affect us all. This exciting field of science has been popularised in the last few years because it explains the rationale behind the theory of the 'law of attraction'. We can manifest what we want by applying our focused intent. Have you read *The Secret* by Rhonda Byrne (2006)? This book is based on the theory that we attract people, situations and experiences into our life based on the frequency that we are vibrating at energetically. Our emotions create a frequency that tunes into other signals on the same frequency. Certainly at a subatomic level, since the 1980s scientists have proved this theory time and time again. In simple terms, our energy flows where our attention goes. Our observation of something will energise the subject being observed. This is why more and more business coaches are recommending the importance of being present and operating in the now. Have you ever been trying to explain something to someone and sensed that although they were physically present, their mind was elsewhere? When you focus all your attention and awareness on an individual, their unconscious mind doesn't just feel it, it literally whoops with delight as their energetic system becomes flooded with an abundance of energy. In her book, *Time to Think*, Nancy Kline (1999) explains that the quality of an individual's listening will determine how intelligently the other person articulates their point. From an energy perspective, focus, presence and intent stimulate and inspire high performance thinking. Gary E. Schwartz is a professor of psychology, medicine, neurology, psychiatry and surgery at the University of Arizona and a man with a passion for lifelong learning. He discovered that the human body acts like a receiver and transmitter of energy, and his findings demonstrate that a simple movement generates an electrical charge that appears to be 'felt' by other people. His theory expanded the view that intention towards someone else has its own physical counterpart, which can be registered by the recipient as a physical effect. Individuals who are sensitive to energy can feel the electromagnetic fields of others who have strong magnetic fields. Robert Jahn at the Princeton Engineering Anomalies Research laboratory and his colleague Brenda Dunne devised a computerised 'heads and tails' test to ascertain whether intention could influence an outcome. Subjects were asked to focus on one option and according to the law of probability they should produce roughly 50 per cent of each option. After 25 years and two and a half million trials they proved that thinking certain directed thoughts could affect an outcome of either 'heads' or 'tails'. Their results were replicated and endorsed by 68 independent investigators. Imagine that you are at a busy airport. There is an assortment of background noises, people talking, walking, pulling luggage, conveyor belts, children crying and sounds of the conveyor belts. Yet mostly you are not bothered by this noise until an announcement calls your flight details and your attention is switched on. Your RAS is the automatic mechanism inside your brain that brings relevant information to your attention. Every living thing has its own unique vibration. Your emotions impact upon your vibration and instruct your awareness to notice where there are similar vibrations to your own in that moment.

Affecting reality with thoughts

My interest in the power of directed thought and how thought can affect physical reality helped me to become aware of the groundbreaking work of Japanese scientist Dr Masaru Emoto, who sadly passed away in October 2014. He became a Doctor of Alternative Medicine at the Open International University for Alternative Medicine in India in 1992, and is known in the alternative medicine realm for his 2005 book, *The Hidden Messages in Water*. Although controversial, Emoto's extensive experiments support his claim that the molecules in water crystals can be directly affected by our thoughts, words and feelings. His water crystal experiments involve dividing water samples taken from the same source into two separate containers, one labelled with positive words such as love and peace, and the other labelled with words associated with negative emotions such as hate, anger and war. These containers, and the water within them, were then frozen, and the water crystals photographed under a microscope. The positive words produced beautiful crystals and the negative words created malformed crystals. Dr Emoto's experiments appear to provide visible proof that thoughts, feelings and intentions really do affect our physical reality. This concept – and its extraordinary implications on performance – can be hard to grasp initially. If you Google Emoto you'll find a plethora of contradictory views, yet traditional scientists are not yet ready to completely dismiss Emoto's work. The impact of Emoto's experiments on your own body is summarised in research published in *Anatomy and Physiology for Nurses: Including Notes on Their Clinical Application* (Pearce, 1975). This highlights that the average adult has 60 per cent proportion of their body weight attributable to water. What if your thoughts affected the symmetry of the water within your body? What if there was a way to discover whether your water structure in crystal formation is symmetrical or misshapen?

The Big Apple Experiment™

As visions of test tube samples of urine and expensive equipment flashed through my mind, I realised I needed to find my own experiment that anyone could do themselves at home or at work in a way that was easy, practical and cheap. I was drawn to using because if you cut an apple widthways you'll see the shape of a pentagram made from the pips. I really warmed to the idea that apples contain my Symbol of Star Quality at their core. Which is why, inspired by Dr Emoto's work, I pioneered the Big Apple Experiment™ as a simple experiment that anybody can do. Sandra Bastin, foods and nutrition specialist, and Kim Henken, extension associate for ENRI, published a chart showing the water content of fruits and vegetables (Bastin and Henken, 1997). Apples have 84 per cent water. I began experimenting to see whether my own thoughts when directed at apples could accelerate or slow down their rate of decay. I started running the Big Apple Experiment™ in 2010. I took an apple and cut it into two halves, placing one half in a glass jar labelled LOVE and the other half in a glass jar labelled HATE. I then spent two weeks speaking in a loving, kind and compassionate way to my LOVE half and shouted verbal abuse to my HATE half. There were moments whilst I was doing this when I did seriously wonder whether I was barking mad. Yet after two weeks I was shocked to see that the HATE apple half was visibly more decayed, was covered with green mould and had shrivelled more than the LOVE apple half. Over the next month my whole house was crammed with apples in glass jars and every visitor and friend I had was asked to participate in this crazy experiment. On 15 March 2010, the *Daily Mail* featured my apple experiment as a double page spread titled 'Could talking to an apple help you become more beautiful?' and it created an overwhelming reaction from the general public – lots of it was not very positive! Radio stations started doing the Big Apple Experiment™ as a joke. Joanne Malin, presenter of the *Breakfast Show* for BBC Radio West Midlands, invited me on air as she revealed the results of her apples following a week of 'apple' rants and raves. Joanne was stunned to see that her directed and verbal abuse had accelerated the rate of decay of one half of her apple and was momentarily speechless. *Heart Breakfast* quickly picked up on this story and television presenter, Matthew Wright, opened one of his episodes of *The Wright Stuff* on Channel 5 with my apple experiment! It was a crazy time because people (including myself) could not understand how or why it worked. I then spent three years encouraging attendees from my charisma seminars to do their own apple experiments and received hundreds of photos showing amazing differences between two halves of the same apple. Could it be that charismatic individuals have the ability to extend the life of an apple by their thoughts, words and intentions? If this surprising theory is correct then charismatic people have the ability to create high levels of well-being within others.

Understanding brainwave patterns

The brain is made up of billions of brain cells called neurones that use electricity to communicate with each other. The combination of millions of neurones sending signals at once produces an enormous amount of electrical activity in the brain, which can be detected using sensitive medical equipment (such as an electroencephalogram (EEG)), measures electricity levels over areas of the scalp. The electrical activity of the brain is commonly called a brainwave pattern, because of its repeating, 'wave-like' nature. These brainwaves can be categorised into:

- Beta – emitted when we are consciously alert, or feel agitated, tense, afraid, with frequencies ranging from 13 to 60 pulses per second.
- Alpha – when we are in a state of physical and mental relaxation, although aware of what is happening around us. This frequency is around 7 to 13 pulses per second.
- Theta – is when we are in a deep trance and have reduced consciousness. This frequency is around 4 to 7 pulses per second.
- Delta – is a deep unconscious sleep or catalepsy, emitting between 0.1 to 4 pulses per second.

In general, we live our daily lives operating with the beta brain frequency. When we slow down our frequency to alpha, we put ourselves in the ideal inner environment to learn new information, retain facts and data, perform elaborate tasks, learn languages and analyse complex situations. Meditation and relaxation exercises will induce the alpha state and this promotes a feeling of calm. According to neuroscientists, who have researched the link between brain rhythms and health, decreasing the brain frequency will increase the levels of beta-endorphins and dopamine (neurotransmitters that make us feel good) and this effect lasts for hours, sometimes even days.

The reason I was interested in brainwave frequencies was to understand whether certain brainwaves were more powerful for creating what you want, manifesting visions and goals and ultimately assessing whether this was an area that could help develop charismatic potential. I soon recognised that there were numerous benefits gained from slowing down brain rhythms to alpha and theta frequencies. Yet many leaders I was working with were known for their speed of thinking and found it difficult to switch off and struggled to slow down. How could I help them to optimise their potential by showing them how to slow down their brainwave patterns as desired?

Impact of frequencies on physical reality

As awareness of my apple experiment grew I met Hugo Jenks, scientist, electronics engineer and author who works within the renewable energy field. He was fascinated by the impact of brainwave patterns on how we feel and how we can consequently affect our physical reality. He introduced me to binaural beat recordings that use specially generated sounds that alter your brainwaves so that they become synchronised with the frequency of the earth's vibration. They are able to promote a profoundly deep state of meditation enabling a greater flow of energy and an increase in neurotransmitters. In 1839 Heinrich Wilhelm Dove discovered the presence of naturally occurring binaural beats – perceived as sounds arising within the brain in response to specific external stimuli. In 1973 Dr Gerald Oster accelerated binaural technology following extensive published studies seeing binaural beats as a powerful tool for cognitive and neurological research. So how does binaural technology work? Two pure tones are produced at slightly different frequencies. When these are listened to simultaneously through headphones, a 'beat' can be perceived as though it were heard. It is not heard by the ear, but only by the processes within the brain. This frequency beat can influence the listener's emotional state through entrainment of brainwaves. Entrainment was initially discovered in 1665 by the Dutch mathematician Christiaan Huygens after he noticed two of his clocks with pendulums began to swing in unison. I immediately saw that Hugo's binaural beat recordings could amplify the impact of hypnosis, meditation and visualisation processes. His recordings were based on frequencies that opened the pathway to the unconscious mind and slowed down the listener's brainwave patterns. I decided to work with Hugo, with two specific areas in mind. First, I decided to run a small trial to identify results from combining binaural beats with my hypnosis scripts and, second, I wanted to see what frequency combination would extend the freshness of an apple. Trials for the efficacy of these blended auditory programmes took place in December 2010 for a two week period and required volunteers to listen to a 12 minute charismatic conditioning programme every day for seven days. Volunteers were asked to rate 20 different emotional states before and after the trial as well as providing qualitative feedback. The trial involved 12 volunteers, 9 women and 3 men, with an average age of just under 48 years. Out of the 20 different emotional states that were measured, 19 of these improved. Volunteers averaged a 32 per cent increase in their energy levels and a 22 per cent improvement in their charisma.

A fresh approach to frequencies

Hugo then conducted his own experiment on my behalf. He worked with three apples. Each apple was cut into two halves and labelled either A or B. All the 'A' apple halves would be subjected to listening to a binaural beat sequence for 30 minutes every day. All the 'B' halves would be left in a different room and would not be subjected to any binaural beat recordings. The first 'A' was exposed to a binaural beat recording that operated at a rhythm of 5 to 10 hertz, the second 'A' at a rhythm of 6 to 15 hertz and the third 'A' at a rhythm of 4 to 13 hertz. The visible conclusion from this one-off experiment was that a binaural beat sequence of 6 to 15 hertz created the freshest apple. This indicated that combining an alpha and theta frequency may have would actively support healing, well-being, inner balance and charisma. This amazing experiment with Hugo helped me to recognise the impact of powerful positive emotions and why slowing down our mind was so beneficial. The emotion of love has a frequency that varies between alpha and theta. Yet most people spend a large proportion of their day operating in a beta frequency! Was this starting to build a case for leaders to adopt a more heart-centred approach?

Frequency range	'A' apple (with binaural beats)	'B' apple (no binaural beats)
5–10 hertz	20% decay	10% decay
6–15 hertz	No decay	40% decay
4–13 hertz	20% decay	90% decay

Control or controlled?

Corporate leaders with a rational, analytical personality demanded that I try to make my experiment more scientific and suggested that I cut the apple into *three* pieces, the extra piece acting as a control. I asked them what they would do with this piece and they said they would ignore it. Strangely, the piece that was ignored was often as decayed as the HATE piece. The impact of neglect is often stronger than hate and the power of love is rejuvenating. I received an apple photo from a top female executive who was going through an acrimonious divorce at the time, who had created the most decay I had ever seen and I seriously worried about the health of her ex-husband. A company specialising in mailing equipment, who were sending people onto my charisma seminars, decided to run the Big Apple Experiment™ with the whole company. Employees were encouraged to 'have a pop' at the HATE apple and 'big up' the LOVE apple. The results were so astonishing that they did the experiment three times with the same success. A well-known holiday company decided to cover their apples with brown bags to heighten the anticipation of the reveal and this became an overnight hit with call centre staff. Executives from all types of organisations kept sending me photos. On one occasion I met Matthew Bent, the owner and CEO of Bents Garden and Home, who is a big believer in positive reinforcement. The work I was doing with apples inspired him to launch The Great Plant Experiment. He set up an experimental bench and encouraged visitors to subject two sets of plants to very different emotions. Six plants were loved with kind words and happy thoughts whilst six plants were subjected to hateful words and emotions. All other conditions such as watering and fertilisation remained the same.

On Twitter Bents Garden and Home announced 'The experiment proved to be popular and the happy side thrived.' The conclusions showed that plants grow bigger and are healthier when they are loved. The public were fascinated by the concept that talking lovingly to their plants keeps them healthy and thriving. Years ago I remember reading an article about Prince Charles talking to plants and at the time thinking he was crazy. Now I recognise that as a huge supporter of the environment he intuitively knows the power of nurture and nourishment.

Success rate

In all honesty, I had no idea how effective this experiment was destined to become because I wondered whether people would be bothered to send me photos of their apple experiments that didn't work. It was only when I launched an in-house version of my seminars – the Charisma Model Programme – that I was able to collect hard evidence based on the number of people who completed the Big Apple Experiment™. Within 12 months we had successfully delivered ten programmes with 114 attendees who were all tasked to complete the Big Apple Experiment™. From the 96 people who did it, 79 per cent got a visible change in their rate of decay between the two apple halves. The photos of people's apple experiments demonstrate that the rate of decay is linked to the intensity and frequency of the negative and positive emotions experienced by each person. If you cannot feel your emotions, if you are not connecting to your emotions, if you have erected an invisible wall around your emotions, then you are probably not going to be able to do the Big Apple Experiment™. The link between your self-awareness, ability to connect emotionally and the intensity and frequency with which you activate your emotions will determine the level of impact you can visibly create on your two apple halves. This experiment enables you to see for yourself that the power of positive thought keeps the LOVE apple fresher and negative thinking accelerates the rate of decay in the HATE apple.

How docs it work?

I did try to find scientific reasons why the Big Apple Experiment™ works and I do recognise that (a bit like the placebo effect) it seems to work better for people that expect it to. Having looked at possible theories ranging from frequencies, intensity, molecular agitation and destructive interference, I gave up trying to explain it. It is not a scientifically controlled experiment, neither am I a scientist, yet it does deliver a powerful metaphor around your ability to create a visible change in your reality based on your focused intent. If you are able to create this level of decay with your words, thoughts and emotions in an apple in just two weeks, just imagine the effect of your own negative self-talk on your body, your family and the people you work with over your lifetime.

The power of prayer

During one of my masterclasses when I was talking about my Big Apple Experiment™ I met a lovely and vibrant woman who was studying to become ordained as a priest. I expressed my concern that it might not feel very spiritual to get in touch with the emotion of hate. She disagreed saying that for her, the LOVE apple represented God and the HATE apple represented the devil. After six weeks she sent me a photo of her apples – her LOVE half still looked amazingly fresh. I realised that when we send love we are effectively praying. According to Albert Szent-Györgyi, in every culture and medical tradition before ours, healing was accomplished by moving energy. I was so blown away by this insight that I studied to become a Reiki Master, recognising that healing is simply a spiritually guided channelling process of life force energy. One of the best designed and rigorous scientific studies I came across that examined the impact of prayer was conducted by the late Dr Elisabeth Targ during the AIDS epidemic in the 1980s. Working with 40 remote healers across America she was able to demonstrate that sending 'healing' improved the health of terminally ill AIDS patients. In 1999 when I completed my Master Practitioner training in neurolinguistic programming (NLP) I met a quirky yet compassionate man, Richard Maczka, former therapist for guests appearing on a daytime TV programme, who had been practising daily meditation for years. He was unable to create any change in his apples because he found it impossible to get in touch with any negative feeling.

Intensity and frequency of your directed intentions

If you are unable to create a visible change in your apples this can usually be attributed to one of three reasons. First, you may not have high levels of negative emotion within you; second, you may not be connecting emotionally; and third, you are not sending your positive and negative intentions out to your apple on a regular enough basis. John Tickner, an engineer who completely understood why my Big Apple Experiment™ worked, explained to me that if you put an apple in a microwave to cook on a low intensity setting for ten seconds it would not have a particularly high impact. If you put an apple in a microwave on a high intensity setting for ten minutes you would be able to see a significant difference in the two apples. So intensity and frequency of your emotional 'zapping' is a key element to the success of your own apple experiment.

The Rotten Apple Syndrome

One morning I remember noticing a rotten apple in my fruit bowl and that same evening I was astonished by the speed that this apple had 'infected' the other pieces of fruit. At work the impact of a disengaged employee spreads contamination faster than a positive and engaged employee can spread inspiration and collaboration. The frequencies of negative and positive emotions are so different that they create a destructive force field (destructive interference) that employees will be consciously and unconsciously receiving. Forward-thinking organisations recognise the value of emotionally intelligent leaders. It is simply a question of time before those same leaders become sensitive to the energy within their working environment. Is it stimulating or draining employee motivation? When people feel understood they are more likely to open themselves up to engaging with the organisation's values. This is why good leaders, charismatic leaders, operate simultaneously from their heart and mind with a positive intent for the well-being of others.

Teaching employees how to work with energy

Every employee is a unique individual. You can't expect an individual to be unaffected by life outside work. Sometimes the noise of ordinary living blocks the labyrinth in our minds. We feel lost in a maze with many twists, turns and exit points that confuse our thinking, and overwhelm our ability to see the good things in life. As we struggle to manage the many facets of our life, we may become acutely aware of the misery and conflict around the world. Instant news hastens more human disaster into our conscious awareness. Whilst I know consciously that how we filter information determines our perception of our reality, the flow and volume of information that streams into our unconscious mind will take its toll. Despite years of working on myself and thousands of pounds invested in my own personal development, I do still find that certain things, certain relationships have the power to cause me huge internal misery and conflict as I fight to restore my inner peace. How can I make sense of a vulnerable little boy being brutally murdered by his mother? How can I begin to understand the terrible death toll of a train crash carrying people on their way to visit one of the most sacred places in Spain? How can I get through to my friend, who is drinking herself into an early grave, believing that she is one of life's victims and her life has been a sad one? Just being human puts us in the centre of our life's experience. Sometimes we have wonderful experiences and at times life can really suck. Therefore, it is impossible to expect an organisation to attain 100 per cent engagement consistently (unless they work at a very superficial level in terms of how they measure it). People are affected by factors outside work as well as within work. Yet their emotional state will distort their perceptions of what is good and what is not so good. Like the apple, if a person is accessing any negative emotion they are creating damage to themselves and others. The only way forward for the enlightened organisation is to equip employees with energy tools, techniques and processes that teach individuals how to choose and control their emotional states.

There are three reasons why I believe you can benefit from doing your own Big Apple Experiment™. First, there is nothing more powerful than seeing the results first-hand. Whilst you may fully embrace the importance of positive thinking, it has become a bit of a theoretical cliché over the years. Doing your own apple experiment can trigger a massive increase of awareness around your own general levels of positivity. The second benefit is more sensory awareness and a stronger connection to your emotions. The ability to access different emotions builds your capability to inspire and engage others. The third benefit is the opportunity to release some suppressed negative emotions that may be blocking your energy and thereby diminishing your overall presence and charisma. Sometimes allowing the release of layers of negative emotions will move you into a growth mechanism.

Step 1 – preparation

Choose your apple, any apple variety will work. Golden Delicious, Granny Smiths, Gala, organic, home-grown, hand-picked from a big superstore or a local farm shop – they all work. Find yourself a couple of glass jam jars with lids and label one jar with a negative emotion you experience on a regular basis. For example, sadness, anger, fear or guilt. Label the other jar LOVE. Take your apple and cut it in half. Place each half into a glass jar and decide where you are going to keep your jars. Ideally, they should be kept in the same room in similar conditions yet far apart so your focused intent towards one jar does not unwittingly impact on the other jar. Both jars are a metaphor for either negative or positive emotions. Many people find it impossible to get in touch with HATE so choose a negative emotion that you can relate to. You can only connect to an emotion if it is within you and you are ready to let it go.

Step 2 – sending negative intentions

Stand in front of your negative jar and think of a time, a specific time when you felt the negative emotion you have chosen to work with. As you think about that time, imagine floating into your younger self who was feeling this emotion. What are you seeing? What are you hearing? What are you saying to yourself? Where in your body do you feel this negative emotion? Does it have a colour and if so what colour is it? Notice whether this negative emotion feels hard or does it feel soft? As you connect fully to this negative emotion within you now notice how it intensifies. Imagine sending all of this negative emotion you have been storing within you into your jar knowing that releasing this negative energy is for your highest good.

Step 3 – sending positive intentions

Stand in front of your 'LOVE' jar and think about someone you really LOVE. Imagine they are standing in front of you now. How are they looking at you? What do you notice about their eyes? As you feel the connection between you both, notice whereabouts in your body you are feeling LOVE. Does this growing feeling of LOVE within you have a colour? If so, what colour is your LOVE? How does this feeling of LOVE feel? What happens if you imagine moving this feeling of LOVE around in a circular movement? If it intensifies, allow this feeling of LOVE to flow around your whole body now and imagine sending all your LOVE to your LOVE jar. Imagine an infinite source of LOVE circling above your head and entering your body now, filling up your whole body with warm LOVING energy. Now imagine this infinite source of LOVE expanding out from your heart into the jar in front of you.

Step 4 – two weeks of support and sabotage

For two weeks spend time loving your LOVE jar and ranting at your negative jar. The more attention you can give to your jars the better the results will be. If you've had a frustrating day at work, why not take your frustrations out on your negative jar? If someone has caused you to feel wonderful for whatever reason, why not imagine their face in your LOVE jar?

Step 5 – your big apple revealed

Open your jars and take out each apple half. Notice the difference in the way each half smells. How do they look? If you want, please take a photo and send it to me; I am really keen to find out how you get on with your own experiment.

Send your apple experiment photos to apples@audiencewithcharisma.com

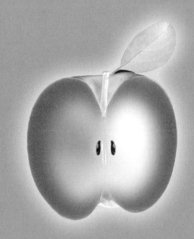

Chapter 10

———

Dismantling your walls

The cell walls were cold to the touch. Lighting from the outside corridor seeped through the gaps around the heavy, locked door, which cast menacing black shadows across the stained mattress in the corner. Prisoner DO2572 shivered. Since the 'incident' a few days ago, she was under 24-hour suicide watch to prevent her from trying to kill herself. Solitary confinement in Holloway Prison. Her body and mind had begun to shut down weeks ago, when they stopped all visits from the outside world and began feeding her through a hatch in the door.

Once a week, the prisoner was escorted to the occupational therapy room where, under the constant vigilance of a prison warden, she was able to lose herself for two hours in painting, writing or some other arts and crafts activity. These weekly sessions, for prisoners deemed to be 'at risk' – either to themselves or to other inmates – were run by a volunteer called Gary. It seemed to the prisoner that Gary's optimism, energy and enthusiasm were completely inappropriate in this miserable place. After a while the prisoner began to trust this man and she started to respond to his encouraging, supportive words. Gary's patience and compassion enabled him to see the good in her. Any evidence of even the smallest effort on her part would be a cause for genuine delight.

The prisoner tentatively started to make a clown, with a knitted head. A happy, smiling, hopeful clown with a yellow hat and pom-poms. The prisoner began to notice the presence of positive emotions where once there had only been despair. As the clown took shape, it became more and more important to her. Every stitch a symbol that she was creating something good out of something bad.

Then something extraordinary happened. Prisoner DO2572 no longer wanted to give up. She began talking to Gary about her feelings, her hopes and her crazy dreams for her future.

When her clown – whom she named 'Holly from Holloway' – was completed she vowed that, if she ever got out of prison, she would make every second of her life count, and over the years 'Holly from Holloway' would become a constant reminder that the gift of hope and self-belief, which Gary had instilled within her, she would give to others.

'Holly from Holloway' is sitting on a ledge in my office and is a little worn and shabby these days – after all she is over 35 years old. Holly reminds me of Gary and his arts and crafts classes. To paraphrase a wonderful quote by Maya Angelou, if I'm honest, I can't quite remember Gary's face, or even the details of what he actually said to me, but I will never forget the way he made me feel. The way that he helped me to see that I had a life worth living. The way that he moved me from an emotional state of utter despair to one of hope. Gary taught me a simple but very important lesson in life. When you feel good about yourself, you feel energised and empowered to do whatever it takes to achieve the results that you want in your life. When you access these emotions you are operating in alignment with your true authentic self and this is the moment when you are at your most charismatic.

Your emotional landscape

Since childhood my favourite book has been *The Secret Garden* by Frances Hodgson Burnett (1911) – I have a first edition that was given to me by my grandmother whom I adored, and just smelling the old print on the pages makes me smile. I loved reading about the sour-faced ten-year-old girl, Mary Lennox, who found a secret and neglected garden that she nurtured back to its full glory. Imagine a neglected garden for a moment. A place full of overgrown weeds that are strangling the life out of beautiful plants that may be completely hidden from view. If the soil has not been turned it cannot create the right conditions for growth. Before you call in the landscape gardener, aren't you curious about discovering what is growing underneath the weeds? I see people with their own emotional landscapes that have become overgrown with the traumas and difficulties they have experienced in their lives. Their gardens are weary from years of neglect and in desperate need of nurturing and weeding. Sometimes the lack of light in the dark recesses of the mind casts menacing shadows that makes it difficult to see the path we are wanting to follow and we may feel lost, isolated and confused. The extraordinarily gifted actor Robin Williams appeared to have it all, a glittering acting career, a loving family, wealth and global recognition. Yet his troubled childhood continued to creep insidiously into his adult life, resulting in depression, addictions and ultimately his suicide when he was only 64. Without addressing the issues from your past, they will continue to have a hold over you, haunting your

Nikki Owen used apples to assess negative impact on poor body image

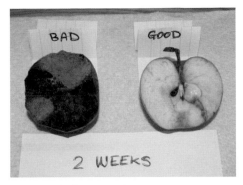

The Head of Finance for an accountancy firm did the experiment for two weeks.

The Metering Communications Manager for a utilities company did the experiment for four weeks.

An ordained priest highlighted the power of prayer when she did her six-week experiment.

An engineer and aviation expert got this result in less than 30 minutes.

The Head of Shared Services for an utilities company did the experiment for 14 days.

Radio WM presenter Joanne Malin did the experiment live on air for seven days.

The Director of People Development and Engagement for a global retail chain did the experiment for seven days.

A 16-year-old girl with body issues did the experiment for six days and triggered a double page feature in *Daily Mail* (Sadie Nicholas, 15 March 2010, *Daily Mail*. 'Could talking to an apple help you to become more beautiful?')

A team leader with a university corporate development unit did the experiment for seven days.

A sales director of global data security company did his experiment for seven days.

The chairman of a CEO group did his experiment for six weeks.

A live two-day experiment at the World of Learning Exhibition 2013.

Senior Solutions Manager for a global holiday company did the experiment for two weeks.

The Head of Learning and Development for a multinational IT organisation did the experiment for three weeks.

The entire workforce from a manufacturer of postage meter and mailroom equipment participated in a six-week experiment.

A demonstration of an experiment during a senior leadership team masterclass.

An emerging leader, worried about her job security, did the experiment for just two weeks.

From left to right (standing): Antony Edwards, Paul Wayman, Sue Bottomley, Jessica Richards, Suz Jeffery, Kevin Dwyer, Angela Tickner, Richard Tickner, Sue Skinner, Corah Clark

Front row: Nikki Owen, Mark Wharton

Sue Bottomley and Jessica Richards photographed whilst channelling Princess Diana and Neferneferuaten Nefertiti. All photos taken during the deep trance session were inexplicably out of focus.

Drawing of Leonardo da Vinci drawn by Mark Wharton with his left hand. Notice the use of mirror writing that was an unusual script favoured by Leonardo da Vinci.

dreams and creating feelings of insecurity, not just within you, within the people you interact with.

Weeding stimulates growth

I believe that we are all born exquisitely perfect; joy is our natural state. We are meant to be happy. Instinctively you know this. Have you ever experienced a feeling of euphoria at the sheer sensation of being alive? This feeling of bliss is our birthright, it is within us all. When we are fully associating to this feeling of bliss we are at our most charismatic. Yet we become increasingly disconnected from this inner joy because of the hurts and tough experiences that build protective walls that block access to an inner serenity. The quickest way to transform how you feel is to make a commitment to 'weed your own emotional garden', because you have an abundance of beautiful flowers and stunning plants within your grasp. You don't need to add in anything extra because you already have all the resources you need inside to feel happy, calm and in balance.

Are you ready to change?

It takes real courage to tackle painful issues from the past. There are three categories of readiness for change. First, most people do not possess a level of self-awareness that enables them to see that they have a need to change. Second, some people may recognise that their 'issues' are holding them back, yet are reluctant to embrace anything that causes them further hurt. Third, there are a small minority of people that recognise they need to change and feel ready and open to wanting to change. When I'm working within organisations, I advise my clients that attending my programmes needs to be a choice. That's why when the Charisma Model Programme is implemented within an organisation, I present what it is to potential attendees so they can decide whether it feels right and appropriate for them. In the past, when I have worked with people on a one-to-one basis, they have experienced such a transformation that they want their wife/husband/employee/partner to work with me. Unfortunately unless this person is ready and willing to embrace change, they will dig in their heels, put up their walls and gain absolutely nothing from their session with me. Are you in the right state of readiness for your own transformation? Reflect on these five areas that are a prerequisite for successful inner change work. Then, you may want to complete the 'Readiness for change' exercise in Appendix 1.

1. Commitment to change

   It's important to know what the proposed changes involve so that you can decide whether or not you are ready and motivated to make those changes. Without this motivation to want to change or without accepting that you have an issue that needs 'fixing', any behavioural changes will be short-lived.

2. Accepting responsibility

   As a child, you were dependent on others for your survival. You became programmed to consider others in the context of how they affect you. You cared what your parents said because they could take things away from you. Part of becoming an adult requires you to accept responsibility for your thoughts, feelings and actions. This helps you to learn from and rectify your mistakes. If you don't take responsibility for the impact your issues are creating on you and others then you're likely to stop growing emotionally. Your adult behaviour then becomes driven by your inner child.

3. Good self-awareness

   When you get hurt, you have a tendency to erect an invisible wall or protective barrier around yourself. Your unconscious mind learns that 'emotions hurt' and you anaesthetise yourself and disconnect from your emotions. Some people who rely mainly on their conscious mind, ignore the whispers from their unconscious mind. This sometimes results in an impaired ability to emotionally connect. Successful change does require a reasonable level of self-awareness and emotional intelligence to 'feel' your emotions in your body.

4. Trusting your unconscious mind

   You instinctively put up invisible barriers when you don't feel safe. In your mind, your barriers protect you. That's why you need to trust your unconscious mind. After all, if you can't trust your unconscious mind whose mind can you trust? Dealing with issues from your past may necessitate a deep change intervention; you need to feel confident that you have the ability to cope with a heightened emotional response to memories that may rise to the surface.

5. Resolving unconscious benefits

Sometimes a barrier to change is a secondary gain, an unconscious benefit that you may not have consciously identified that keeps you 'chained' to your issue. Once identified, if the benefits from the secondary gain outweigh the negative consequences of the issue, then the potential for sustainable change is hampered. For example, a businessman I worked with about his anger issues towards his father, believed he achieved high levels of business success to prove to his father that he was 'good enough'. In his mind he had linked his anger to the reason for his driving force and business success. He was concerned that by taking away the anger towards his father he might take away his drive and determination. I worked with a woman who worked with homeless young people and suffered with chronic back pain. She found juggling the demands of a full-time job and looking after the family exhausting. She was able to rest after work because her partner insisted that he dealt with the children and did the cooking. In her mind her chronic back pain created the space for her to rest. Another person I worked with had ME. They found the pressure of their work overwhelming and recognised that if they did get well they would need to work long and stressful hours. With ME they could work at a pace that they determined rather than fall short of their manager's high expectations. One of the funniest examples of a secondary gain was demonstrated by my daughter's seven-year-old dog, Mindy, a tiny little Yorkshire terrier. Several weeks ago, Mindy stumbled up the steps to the front door and damaged her front right leg. We took her to the vet, who confirmed that there was no lasting damage, perhaps just a bruise or a strain. Nevertheless we made a huge fuss of Mindy. We found ourselves routinely lifting her on and off settees, and carrying her home when, with a pathetically upraised right paw, she signalled to us that the daily walk had all got a bit too much for her. I am pleased to report that Mindy's leg is much better now, and has even passed 'the squirrel test' on two separate occasions, when she runs like the wind in an attempt to catch them. However, from time to time (and almost always when she is on her own in another room), Mindy has developed the habit of letting out a loud, distressed squeal, accompanied by an upraised paw. This squeal is traumatic enough to cause the entire household to rush to her aide, pick her up and fuss her, at which point she has now added a very convincing and uncontrollable tremor to her symptoms! After a minute or two of our undivided attention she is, of course, perfectly fine again.

Charisma is self-acceptance

Charisma is not something you can add to your skill set, it is a deep reconnection with who you truly are at your core. To want to be more charismatic requires a commitment to clear away the debris left in the emotional wake of living your life. One of the biggest mistakes people make when they commit to creating change within themselves is that they try to change what they see as their faults and imperfections into strengths and positive qualities. The best way to build your own authentic charisma is to accept yourself for who you are. Allowing yourself to experience a 'moment of acceptance' means that you stop resisting your current predicament. This doesn't mean that you stop trying to improve your life. It just means that when you face up to the full reality of your challenges, and stop trying to resist them in a rigid, adversarial way, you allow the universal wisdom to guide and support you until you have found your way back to you. Acceptance of you as you are, acceptance of your life enables you to go with the flow in the knowledge that trying to swim against the tide is stressful and exhausting.

Negative programming

If you do not have a good self-esteem, then it's time you worked on having a better image of yourself – because this will improve the overall quality of every aspect of your life. Negative experiences in childhood are often particularly damaging to self-esteem. In your early years your personality and sense of self is being formed, and harmful experiences can leave you feeling that you are not valued or important. The same event experienced through the eyes of a child and through the eyes of an adult will be perceived differently. As a child you have not had a chance to build up any resilience, so one negative experience can create a raft of limiting and negative attitudes that may unwittingly sabotage your adult behaviour. Significant traumatic experiences in your adult life can also instil limiting beliefs and buried negative emotions.

Lessons from the past

Your self-esteem is determined purely by the way you perceive yourself on a 'not good enough–more than good enough' continuum. If you see yourself as lacking, then how can you expect to access your charisma? It took me years to recognise that punishing myself, and being a harsh critic of everything I was and did, was simply not helping me to feel like a worthwhile person who could enhance rather than wreck lives. Like everyone, I have gone through some difficult times, tough experiences that were traumatic and troubling. I know that my past can never change. I can only change my perception of my past. If I am able to see that every negative experience gave me a positive lesson that accelerated my personal development, then this enables me to let go of negative and damaging attachments. Your past isn't the issue; it is the negative emotional responses that certain events in your past evoke that are the real problem. Your past is just a story. And once you realise this it has no power over you. Every thought is a creation. You are alive right now and are creating all of the time. What you believe you are is just your point of view, your story about your perception of you and your past, and perceptions can change. When we over-think things we hamstring our ability to take more ownership of our feelings. Our thoughts become the voice of all knowledge. If that 'voice' is destructive it will create neurosis as we nail ourselves to the cross of our own fiction. We are the main character in a story we have scripted ourselves, yet our past is in the past. If we allow our story to create fear or judgement about ourselves, then we are working out of harmony with our true spirit.

Fight or flight response

Further advocates of the damage our negative programming can do include cellular biologist Dr Bruce Lipton. He states that the self-esteem, values and beliefs from our parents (or the people who brought us up) have been instilled within us by the time we are six years old. These may support, empower or sabotage our thinking and behaviour as adults. Part of our evolution comes from experiencing challenges, obstacles, difficulties and traumas. The healthy way to deal with these 'difficulties' is often referred to as the fight or flight response – intended to help you to survive a dangerous situation by preparing you to either run for your life or fight for your life. Fear – and the fight or flight response in particular – is an instinct that every animal possesses. Gazelles in the Serengeti will have numerous life and death chases as predators are continually hungry and on the prowl for food. After surviving the jaws of a hungry lion, gazelles will shake uncontrollably because this is their natural way of shaking off the excess adrenalin their fear has evoked. Yet what about people? Unfortunately, most of us have lost this natural instinct to 'shake off' our fears and traumas.

Freeze response

Many of us 'freeze' and bury our responses along with all the associated negative emotions and limiting beliefs. According to traditional Chinese medicine, we have 20 meridians – these are like pathways that channel life energy known as Qi (pronounced 'Chee') to every organ in our body. Each buried emotional issue causes a blockage within our meridian system and starts to build a volcano of stored negativity. This creates an imbalance within our body that weakens our immune system and starts a pattern of self-sabotaging actions. Holding onto these issues becomes exhausting. Imagine trying to hold a beach ball full of air under water for any length of time. The drain on your physical strength and energy will cause you to experience emotional outbursts as you 'release the ball'.

Emotional Freedom Techniques

One evening in early January 2011, I was staying with close friends when the conversation turned to Emotional Freedom Techniques (EFT), or 'tapping' as it is more frequently called. My friend, Ted, had just qualified as a practitioner and was explaining that this fast evolving process was like psychological acupressure. The technique works by releasing blockages within the energy system that are the source of emotional intensity and discomfort. These blockages challenge us emotionally, often leading to limiting beliefs and behaviours and an inability to live life harmoniously. EFT involves the use of fingertips rather than needles to tap on the end points of the main meridians that are situated just beneath the surface of the skin. It is non-invasive and works on the ethos of making change as simple and as pain free as possible. In the short time since its inception by Gary Craig in the 1990s, EFT has provided thousands of people with relief from all manner of problems and conditions, often in a startlingly quick time. Ted gave me my first experience of tapping, which resulted in accessing a memory of when my mum had accidentally dropped me down some steps when I was eight months old. It was extremely emotional, life-changing and took just 30 minutes – I was flabbergasted! I wanted to be able to do this. I trained with Karl Dawson as an advanced practitioner of EFT and his powerful memory reframing process, Matrix Reimprinting, and started using these techniques whenever a vague opportunity presented itself. I craved practice opportunities in the same way that I crave water after an intense workout. Malcolm Gladwell (2009) in his book, *Outliers: The Story of Success*, and Matthew Syed's (2010) book, *Bounce – How Champions are Made*, challenge the 'talent myth'. They reject the concept of genetic predisposition and put forward a compelling case to support the view that top achievement is the consequence of huge amounts – 10,000 hours to be precise – of 'purposeful' practice. I had an insatiable desire to practise on everyone – I was like a demon possessed as I practised on family, friends, people at networking events, my audience after my keynote speeches, even random strangers I met on trains – until I attained a level of self-confidence and high levels of competence that enabled me to start blending this technique with the other approaches and modalities I had learned over the years. Realising that EFT activated a trance-like state, I used my knowledge as a hypnotherapist to leverage and accelerate the depth I was able to work at, so my clients were able to reach into the real recesses of their suppressed unconscious. In my quest to identify the root cause behind each client's presenting issues, I started to incorporate Time Line Therapy, which I had learned with Tad James in California in 2000. This opened up the field to work with individuals who had less self-awareness. After becoming a Reiki Master I incorporated Reiki and enlisted the power of a transcendental team (profuse thanks to

Dr Usui, Dr Hayashi and Mrs Takata) and this had a phenomenal impact on the results I was getting for each client I worked with. If you don't know much about Reiki, it is simply using your directed, focused intention to send love and healing energy (called Ki, pronounced 'Key', in Japanese) either to yourself or someone else. I started using more of my NLP techniques when I reframed unhelpful ways of viewing the world with an array of innovative techniques. Having completed over 2,000 different sessions with a wide range of people with varying personality types, I then introduced a condensed version to attendees during my charisma seminars at the Globe Theatre. The charisma team who supported me throughout my two-day event went through a rigorous training and accreditation process in my blended approach, so that collectively we were able to offer attendees an even deeper experience. The changes we created in two days were so remarkable that when our attendees returned to work, their colleagues and bosses were so impressed with the difference they would book themselves onto the charisma seminar.

Repairing my piggy bank

When working at this depth with so many people, I noticed that their issues were mirroring and often triggering many of my own hidden emotional issues. I became the participant in an intense and accelerated phase of personal development, amazed at how much 'stuff' and emotional baggage of my own I was carrying. Within my team we often did swop sessions for each other and I vividly remember one of my own extraordinary and life-changing sessions. I'd had a cavalier attitude towards money for most of my life. During my career I had earned a good salary and I had an incredible appetite for spending it. I would commit my own business to high annual overheads, I was excessively generous with friends and family and on occasions I felt an overwhelming compulsion to spend money. Coincidentally, during an interview on Dr Miriam Stoppard's television show in the early 1990s, I met and then became friends with the daughter of Viv Nicholson who had won £152,319 in 1961 on the football pools and had spent the lot. Looking back, I justified this need to spend with the knowledge that the traumas I had experienced in my teens had affected my self-esteem. I thought I was desperately seeking validation that I was a worthy member of society. Surrounding myself with expensive material possessions demonstrated to myself and others that I was successful. Little did I know that the real root cause of my desire to spend money went much deeper than that. When I was six years old, an angry friend of the family smashed my little china piggy bank during a violent outburst of temper. The combination of his shouting and witnessing the breaking of china and all my pocket money falling to the floor caused me to feel extremely frightened. I instantly formed the belief, 'it's not safe to save money'. I then decided to recreate this memory differently in my own mind and so had my mum, dad, sister and brother all sitting around the dining room table, sticking all the pieces of my piggy bank back together. Even though I knew consciously what had really happened, this recreation gave my six-year-old self resolution and a sense of peace: mending my broken piggy bank in my mind had repaired my damaging belief about saving money. Even though I had completely suppressed this memory over the years, this belief had unconsciously driven my attitude to money, saving and spending as an adult. The newly reimprinted memory has transformed my attitude towards money. I have a savings account, I choose to pay bills quickly and always operate in credit. The emotional urge that I used to feel about buying things has disappeared and consequently my home and wardrobe are a lot less cluttered. This incident helped me to realise just how much of our negative programming was created in childhood. If I had gone to see a conventional counsellor about my spending habits I doubt we would have located the root cause.

Revisiting old memories

Every time you revisit an unpleasant memory you change that memory because you create a tiny pattern interrupt that distorts the link between the memory and negative emotions. Revisiting memories whilst tapping (applying EFT techniques) will induce a light trance-like state. This means that you are working with the unconscious mind where you can be most effective. This trance-like state is evidenced in the body with a slight watering in the eyes, arm catalepsy and deeper breathing. Your various younger selves have beliefs and values based on their experience of life up until that point. Be aware that when revisiting memories where you see your 'younger' self in the picture, you are disassociating from your emotions. If you are experiencing it through your own eyes you are associating with your emotions. When working with your younger 'selves' your first priority is to ensure they feel safe and protected. When working with memories, because you are working with your unconscious mind, without ego, people in your memories tend to be more understanding and helpful.

When does coaching become therapy?

Within organisations, the mantra 'coaching is not therapy' is frequently stated in training programmes about coaching. Yet the distinction between coaching and therapy can be difficult to articulate for many coaches – especially those who are new to the field or who have been previously trained as a psychotherapist specialising in short-term therapy. In the course of coaching, clients may present life patterns that exceed the parameters of coaching. Coaching theory identifies two core differences between coaching and therapy based on primary function and time frames:

1. The primary function of coaching is to create a context in which life and performance development may take place. Coaching assumes that the client is already high functioning and is capable of taking consistent action steps towards their life vision. EFT and Matrix Reimprinting focus on the barriers that are preventing high functioning, so this appears to contradict the primary function of coaching. Coaching works in the 'critical gap' between the present and the client's vision of their future. In coaching, the client's history is approached only as the map that brought the client to the present situation.

2. The primary function of therapy is to create a context in which healing may take place. Therapy assumes that symptoms or behavioural patterns need to be fixed, that something in the client needs to be healed. EFT and Matrix Reimprinting work by identifying the root cause of the presenting issue and helping the individual release and resolve negative emotional attachments and limiting beliefs relating to their issue, rather than trying to 'fix' the issue. Based on the primary function of therapy, EFT and Matrix Reimprinting still fit more into the therapy rather than coaching category. Therapy tends to work either in the past to promote emotional healing or resolve psychological pain, or in the present to reduce destructive patterns.

Emotional causes behind critical illness

The body is extremely responsive to emotions. Suggestions given when you are in a heightened emotional state will create a powerful and lasting impact. A dynamic CEO of a manufacturing company asked me to work with his group IT director who had, at the age of 44, suffered a heart attack. Although he had been given the all-clear by his heart surgeon he was apprehensive that his heart might suddenly stop. He was incredibly anxious and kept nervously covering his heart with his hand. It transpired that both his parents had died young from heart failure and I initially thought that this was the root of his fear. Once I had managed to release the huge amounts of fear he had suppressed, he was able to revisit a memory that he had not consciously recalled in years. He spoke of being six and sitting in the garden with his friends. He recalls discussing how they were all going die and at what age. His friend decided that the number of their house would be the age of their death. My client lived at number 44 and had his heart attack at age 44. I am constantly amazed at the power of a childhood memory. He recently sent me a photo of him celebrating his 45th birthday during his 'glad to be alive' party. The CEO was simply grateful to have his group IT director, fighting fit and back at work.

Therapeutic interventions in a business environment

Psychometric testing provides a powerful way of ensuring the best candidates are selected for positions by assessing their ability and preferred behavioural styles. If an organisation uses assessment tools before they recruit candidates, why would that same organisation not help the individual look at the factors in their past that may be blocking their potential to perform effectively? Many organisations have developed key competencies for different job roles and these competencies are generally categorised as knowledge, skill or behaviours. Sustainable behavioural change can only be consistently created by shifting or changing the person's attitude. If a behaviour is not aligned with the individual, they will struggle to demonstrate the behaviour. If the individual's behaviour is not aligned to the organisation's vision, then how can you change their behaviour in a way that is appropriate and beneficial to the individual as well as the organisation? Trying to change behaviour consciously is difficult and doomed to failure because past programming drives our unconscious behaviours.

An explosive reaction

An international pharmaceutical company had recently acquired a smaller competitor and were making a number of staff redundancies. One of the operations managers had attended my masterclass and requested a follow up one-to-one session with me. His presenting issue was that he felt extremely concerned about the livelihoods of the staff he was making redundant and was struggling with handling this aspect of his job role. I sensed something deeper and I have learned to trust and be patient when working with EFT and Matrix Reimprinting. Just as the session was finishing, his unconscious mind took him back to a previous job where he worked in a fireworks factory. He was involved in a massive explosion that broke his leg and killed his best friend. I will never forget this moving session as he cried and shook uncontrollably for nearly an hour. Then his grey pallor turned to a pinkish hue and he became calm, peaceful and relaxed. I felt I had witnessed a type of emotional exorcism. In a way I had because this trauma had been tormenting him for years. Days later he emailed to tell me that he felt fantastic, he was sleeping soundly at night and his wife and daughter could not believe the change in him. At work he showed compassion with the way he handled the scheduled redundancy programme and his anxieties about the process were completely appropriate for what was going on. Whilst this session was in truth a therapy session, his buried trauma was impacting on his work as well as home life.

EFT and Matrix Reimprinting therapies are gaining momentum in their exposure, and thousands of people are finding that in just a few sessions they can release the demons that currently haunt their past. The more negative programming you are currently living with, the less charisma you can access. Buried issues and traumas create walls and block the real authentic you from emerging. As strange as it sounds, you can boost your presence by releasing your past issues. This therapeutic intervention process is one I have used successfully in a business environment for years because it is the quickest way to create sustainable behavioural change. The biggest changes I have witnessed have been when I have been using EFT and Matrix Reimprinting. As a starting point my suggestion is to do some online research to review the opinions of various experts and authorities. There are plenty of video demonstrations on YouTube and if you visit the Association for Advanced Energy Techniques (AAMET) you'll find a number of accredited practitioners listed on their website. As an energy releasing tool it is easy to learn so please visit my EFT for Self tutorial on my website nikkijowen.com/releasestress

Chapter 11

The charismatic mindset

During my years of studying and working with charismatic individuals I have identified eight powerful guiding principles that create the right conditions for your charisma to flourish. As you read through and become familiar with these beliefs you may find it interesting to notice the way your emotional guidance system responds. You may find that some of these principles really resonate with you, making sense at a deep level. You have no idea why you accept them, you just do. Then you may find others cause you to feel sceptical or even angry. If this happens, then pause for a moment and ask yourself why? What is it about this particular set of words, this statement, that has stirred up your emotions? The time when we grow most is when we feel uncomfortable because we are being stretched to think and act in another way. These beliefs may challenge what you may have held to be true for years and can shake up your reverie of the 'truths' you have been living with until this point.

1. The world is just an illusion; we only ever experience an incomplete perception of what is out there. Miracles happen if you are willing to stop struggling and allow them into your life. You can change anything by changing your thoughts.

   According to Albert Einstein when it comes to your thoughts and attitudes, 'If there is no freedom inside here, there is none elsewhere' (Einstein and Infeld, 1938). Regardless of whether a belief has scientific evidence to support it or not, your beliefs affect your perception of reality. One change in your thinking can have a profound and seemingly miraculous affect on your reality. I recently worked with a tough and fiercely independent woman in her 50s who was working in a senior position within a utilities company. During an in-house programme I was running for leaders, she appeared disengaged and resistant to my methods, describing me quite openly as 'barking as a box of frogs'. I was strongly aware of the steel wall she had erected around herself and she radiated an undercurrent of anger. She was angry at everyone: people at work, previous boyfriends, parents and even a fairly mild and reasonable request was met with an aggressive barb. She had no idea how angry she was. Looking at the world through her eyes, it was a cold, tough and unjust place. She felt attacked, coerced and cornered. This was her reality, as seen through the eyes of anger. After an intensive one-to-one session, she became astonished at how many people were there in her life, offering support. When she connected with her true self, the walls that had been keeping others at bay disappeared with seemingly miraculous results. If you are aware of a struggle within your own life, recognise that you may be trying to fight the natural state of flow desired by your true authentic self. What is it you need to pay attention to that you are currently not noticing? If your perception of your world changes, then your world changes in ways that can often appear miraculous. Because of the causal chain reaction from a single thought, becoming more mindful, more aware of the thoughts you are thinking is vital. If it feels right then it generally is the right path for you.

2. Attitudes of optimism and positivity are not accidents, they are learned skills.

A positive attitude will lead to positive outcomes in all areas of your life and conversely a negative attitude will lead to negative outcomes. What you believe has a powerful influence over your body, your relationships and your environment. You weren't born with a negative attitude; it is a learned response to your life's experiences. What you focus your mind on becomes your reality; your thoughts inspire action, action leads to habit and habit creates your destiny. *Horizon* produced a powerful documentary for BBC Two called 'The Truth about Personality'. Its presenter, Michael Moseley, explored whether personalities can be changed. As a pessimist he frets about the future, finds it difficult to sleep and worries about the smallest little thing. Using two simple techniques that trained his brain to perceive things differently, he proved that in just three weeks his negative thinking reduced and he felt more empowered and positive. Most of our thoughts are unconscious and many of these are negative. Some of these thoughts trickle or even flood into our conscious awareness. These negative thoughts and feelings are very damaging. The first step in changing those in your conscious mind is to become more aware of them. The rubber band exercise mentioned at the end of Chapter 2 is a great way to changing the way you think. This exercise begins to interrupt your ability to 'do' negative thoughts. Since habits grow stronger with time and many experts agree that it takes 21 days to establish a habit, it is possible to change unwanted attitudes if you consistently and regularly become consciously aware of them. During my one-to-one sessions, I sometimes create a picture of a tree with leaf-shaped Post-it notes to map out a person's history of significant events. As they look at their 'tree of life' they start to recognise recurring themes and self-sabotaging patterns. Often just having this awareness creates a change in their thinking and attitude. Everyone has an innate ability to shine, so why do some people shine more brightly than others? Every time you experience hurt, fear, anger, grief or guilt and you remain unaware of these negative emotions, they form into mountainous stores of suppressed negativity that can erupt, like a volcano, at any time. This suppressed negativity, locked away in your unconscious mind, blocks your energy and tarnishes your natural shine. Over time if you learn to suppress more and more of your natural emotional responses, you begin to operate like an automaton in a grey twilight world filled with stress, pressure, barriers and deadlines. Jacintha Saldanha, the British nurse who tragically committed suicide after taking a prank call from an Australian radio show believing it was from the royal family, demonstrated that, left unchecked, stored negative emotions will eventually erupt. To many people who read about this sad case, Jacintha's extreme behaviour must have been difficult to understand. Yet to Jacintha this was the only course of action she must have believed to be available. Many of us experience reactions that are out of proportion to what is actually happening in the present because something has triggered a memory or memories from the past. This is why we need to hold compassion in our hearts for people like Jacintha, rather than judging them from our own perception of how we would respond. Becoming mindful of your thoughts and noticing whether they support or sabotage your outlook is a vital step when evolving yourself into a positive happy person.

3. You have to dare to lose to win. A life without risk is a life not fully lived.

This principle was inspired by Sven-Göran Eriksson, who taught me about taking risks, I fully embrace the importance of stretching myself outside my comfort zone. I remember my mum telling me that she didn't want to reach her 70s regretting things she never did. I have learned so much during some of the toughest and scariest times in my life. One of my friends has lived all his life in the same town and, even though he is in his 50s, has remained in the same house for over 25 years. He has stayed in a job he doesn't enjoy for over 20 years and returns to the same holiday destinations, year after year. Despite inheriting a bit of money and desperately needing a bigger house as his two children are growing up, he feels more comfortable holding onto his money just in case he might need it in the future. His preferred topic for conversations is around times in his past. Whenever I see him I feel intensely sad because his life force appears weak and grey. His infrequent smile rarely touches his eyes and he looks exhausted by the pressure of keeping safe, secure and protected. Every change you choose to make in your life will create a difference in your life. Sometimes that difference may be positive for you and sometimes not. Yet remaining within your comfort zone will deaden your senses over time as your system, which thrives on stimulation, starts to close down. The aura of your life starts to possess a greyish tinge, which suppresses the joy of living life to the full because playing it safe will suffocate your soul. If you do not yet have the courage to take a risk or feel concerned about losing what you already have then your mindset switches into a survival mechanism. This closes off your opportunities for growth. When you recognise that nothing ever stays the same, that there is a constant flow that continually urges you to change, you may find it easier to accept that the biggest risk to your personal happiness is your desire to not take risks.

4. The majority of illness is initially created from an emotional trauma that has been frozen and hidden within a person's unconscious mind. When you release emotional trauma you begin to heal. When you know what to look for, a person's body will indicate clues to their emotional disposition.

I have noticed that many of today's leaders are becoming more disciplined with their health and fitness. There is a growing trend in corporate life towards the belief that a healthy body creates a healthy mind. Your body is truly your friend because it gives you feedback about what's really going on in the inside. Many ancient healing systems, including that advocated by Hippocrates, the father of Western medicine, recognise the role that emotions play in health and physicality. In the 1920s Harvard scientist Walter Cannon MD identified the fight or flight response and the damage that long-term stress can do to the body. David Hamilton, who spent four years in the pharmaceutical industry developing drugs for cardiovascular disease and cancer, found that men in happy marital relationships, who have undergone major heart surgery, heal more quickly.

Louise Hay, founder of Hay House Publishing, believes that every thought we think is creating the fabric of our existence and our thoughts and emotions will ultimately show up in our bodies. When you feel in balance emotionally you support your body's natural blueprint for perfect health. When you are stressed, out of balance or start to suppress your emotions you will notice a deterioration in your physical health. If you continue to ignore these early signs you may develop a more serious illness. You can learn so much just from observing people. Every part of your body can act as an indicator of the emotional imbalance that people experience. For example, your eyes are the way you see your world. Is it possible that short-sightedness is simply a person's unconscious reaction to not wanting to see something clearly? A friend of mine with five children has gone through years of abusive relationships – her marriage and subsequent relationships were typified by rows, accusations and physical violence. Her youngest daughter now wears hearing aids in both ears because she has lost 70 per cent of her hearing. What young child wants to listen to their mummy and daddy rowing all the time? She has effectively switched off the sound of their heated and volatile discussions. From the age of 11, I suffered chronic migraines that were so bad they would keep me in a darkened room for three days. I couldn't eat, think straight or read because the pain was so intense. Years later I recognised that I had unconsciously created these migraines as a way of forcing my body to rest. In the past I would push myself to the point that I physically couldn't work and had to rest. I no longer have migraines because I now listen more carefully to my body's feedback. In my 40s I was in an intense relationship with a man who had just come out of a 24-year marriage where he had felt deeply unhappy. He was diagnosed with diabetes – what a great metaphor about lacking sweetness in your life! He decided that because he felt happy he didn't need to 'do diabetes anymore'. His GP was more than a little surprised. I'm not saying that it's this easy to heal physical issues because it may take years for an individual to even feel open to the concept that their health can be dramatically affected by their mind.

5. When another person creates a strong negative response within you, your unconscious mind is announcing that this is 'your' issue and it wants to deal with it now.

As I've grown older I have learned to become more tolerant and accepting of other people's behaviour. I am generally able to connect at some level with most people, yet every now and then I come into contact with someone who 'brings up my stuff'. I believe that when this happens there is a reason why we have unconsciously attracted this person into our reality at this particular time. In 2011 my success as a speaker was growing rapidly and I wanted to be coached and mentored by one of the UK's top speakers. I had heard that this individual had a reputation for being extremely tough and challenging. I arrived at his house and was greeted by his PA who quickly asked me if I wanted to pay for the session beforehand. That grated with me a bit because I saw it as quite 'money grabbing'. When this guy finally walked into the room he started a one way monologue that criticised my marketing collateral, my biography information, my website and my 'pretty' publicity photos. I remember trying really hard not to cry and left the session feeling as if I was a complete and utter failure. Initially I was really angry with this man who I saw as rude, egotistical, a bully and completely useless as a coach. Then, after a few days, I began to realise that for years I had at a deep level believed that *I was a failure*. This man had actually done me a huge favour. Whether it was intentional or not he had helped me to tackle and resolve an issue that had been lurking in the dark shadows of my unconscious mind for years. I think this happens to many people. The people who trigger a strong and negative emotional response within us are simply holding up a mirror. Now when this happens to me I know I am about to deal with some past issues. Difficult and challenging people are your personal tutors who are putting you through a life simulation to help you grow. There may be recurring patterns that emerge that link many of your difficult relationships. I've worked with leaders who find their vision has been hampered by some 'short-sighted and ignorant' chairmen. It surprises them that their chair has unwittingly evoked memories of an abusive and controlling father. When you change the way you look at someone you see their shortcomings differently. My oldest girlfriend has experienced three violent relationships with men who were all heavy drinkers. She can't believe how unlucky she is – out of all the available men on the planet, how come she 'attracts' the aggressive ones? Over the years her own drinking has increased and she is currently receiving treatment for alcoholism. People with drink problems like to mix with people who drink – was it her relationships that caused her to drink or her own drink-related problems that attracted these three men into her life? When you transmit and receive information on a vibrational frequency, this is based on the emotions you are feeling. Therefore you can only connect with or operate within the parameters of this frequency. So if someone enters your life and creates a negative response within you, then it highlights that their issue is an issue that you, too, possess. We project our own issues, challenges and problems into our external world so our external world gives us continual feedback about the issues we need to resolve next. In my own relationships I was with a man whom I regarded as my soulmate for eight years. He believed he wasn't good enough for me and ultimately his belief sabotaged our relationship and it ended. I felt really angry with him and went to see my coach/therapist to work out what was really going on. During the session I recognised that I had tended to choose men who I believed would be less demanding of me because I truly thought that when they got to know me they wouldn't like me. I believed that I couldn't sustain a long-term relationship because my partner would get bored with me. I then saw that I needed to feel in control of the men I was with so they wouldn't leave me. In a way I *was* choosing men that weren't what I really wanted because I didn't think I could attract *those* types of men! When you uncover a belief at this depth it does shake up your world. This awareness would not have happened without the issues arising from my own dysfunctional relationship.

6. Whenever we blame luck, other people, our childhood, our circumstances for the things that happen, we instantly disempower ourselves and send an unspoken message that we have a victim mentality.

Many of us have experienced tough times during our lives. People may have hurt us (physically or emotionally), we may have been ill, been made redundant, experienced grief at the loss of a loved one or struggled to cope financially. If we blame others for how we feel now, then we disempower ourselves. By pushing the problem onto someone else we also push away our ability to resolve or solve that problem. By acting as a victim we automatically block the possibility of change. In life you will only ever manifest one of two different outcomes. You will either create the results you want in your life or you have reasons why you didn't create the results you wanted. Where you place your awareness determines what you energise and give life to. Focusing on the reasons means you become really good at reasons and this makes it harder to move towards your desired results. Given that the only reality you have is the one you create inside your head, then a reality of 'excuses' will create a different vibe when contrasted to a reality of 'results'. Whilst I know and believe this I do occasionally find myself wallowing in a bucket of self-pity when I seek to blame everyone else for my perceived misfortune. This is a luxury that I can't afford to indulge in for very long because energetically it drains me, causes me to feel overwhelmed and places me in the frequency of 'victim'. Whatever emotional state you find yourself in, notice what it is, then aim to choose an emotional state that feels happier. Realistically it's challenging to transcend from fear into a glorious state of bliss – the jump in frequency is too much. Yet choosing hope or acceptance is perhaps easier to access and will set you on the right path. A mantra that I also use during tough times is a saying, 'It is what it is – all will be well.' It's amazing how quickly you can change how you feel when you change your inner voice. I remember meeting Neale Donald

Walsch, bestselling author of the Conversations with God series. He posed the question, 'What if every difficulty we experience in our life is giving us the opportunity to experience a higher version of ourselves?' When you can face failure and disappointment through the eyes of responsibility then you are unconsciously accepting that your destiny is in your hands. That's empowering for you and empowering for others.

7. When helping others, change will not be possible unless the individual is prepared to accept full responsibility for their life. When an individual is ready to change, they will. If you try to help someone to change before they are ready, their walls of resistance will block change from occurring.

Doing the work that I do, I am really driven to do whatever I can to help people by trying to 'fix' them. However, each of us will only make a decision to change once we are ready to change. That change will remain continually out of reach unless we are prepared to accept responsibility for our situation. I remember working with a business development director who was excellent at building strong relationships with clients, yet was rude and opinionated with people in her office. Her CEO suggested we work together and right from the start she held the belief that, apart from the directors, the rest of the people where she worked were useless and incompetent. She was not taking any responsibility for the atmosphere she was so clearly contributing to at work. As I tried working with her it became clear that she wanted others to change to conform to her way of working. She was judgemental and intolerant about anything other than 'her way'. It was one of the longest sessions I have ever done because I tried every technique, skill and tactic to see if I could get her to soften and change her viewpoint. Regardless of my efforts, nothing worked. Initially I felt defeated that I had not created a significant change for her and her CEO, yet it was a great lesson that people only change when they are ready and wanting to change. The outcome of this session meant that I am much more thorough in checking out people's readiness for change. Sometimes my approach is not right for an individual and sometimes I'm not the right person to help an individual. When I started running the Charisma Model Programme within organisations, rather than as open programmes at The Globe, my first client was a southern-based utilities company. The vision and passion from the head of people development helped me to better position what I do with internal leaders. Mandy spoke about people being 'ready' for such a different type of programme and together we decided that attendance needed to be voluntary rather than mandatory. The results I had delivered were so impressive that the CEO and the rest of the executive management team wanted to implement the programme with every leader and individual flagged as talent or high potential. Despite the lucrative size of this contract on the table, I insisted it was only offered to people who wanted to attend. My approach is challenging enough for individuals who are ready and if a person doesn't want to be there it will create more resistance. Think about the times in your own life when you've felt resistant to change. What was the catalyst that caused you to change? Maybe the pain of your current situation became intolerable or maybe you had a glimpse into what you could have or be that compelled and drove you to change. Within an organisational context, the role of the leader is to convey a strong reason why the planned changes will be beneficial. Whilst these changes may be happening regardless of workforce attitudes, when people feel engaged and open, any changes will be accelerated through any valley of despair into the whole new way of doing things. That is why your charisma becomes a vital component in announcing, managing and implementing successful change.

8. Consciously or unconsciously we learn from our parents in two distinct ways: we either strive to emulate their behaviour and values or we vow to do and think the complete opposite. Either way we should acknowledge and be grateful for the gift we received from our parents.

   In business, stored negativity that may have started in childhood causes disengagement on a breathtaking scale that infects and erodes energy. The parental relationship is often replayed within an organisational context, where we may unknowingly perceive colleagues, line managers or leaders as manifestations of our father or mother because something about their behaviour, the way they look or how they speak triggers us back to our past. The study of neuroscience has identified that the amygdala, located deep within the medial temporal lobes of the brain, is responsible for triggering fear. If an organisation unwittingly triggers a negative 'parental relationship' emotion, the individual will be plunged into anxiety, stress and survival mode. The quickest and most effective way to combat this unhelpful reaction is to understand the positive 'gifts' we received from our parents, either directly or indirectly. When we can 'let go' of old parental relationship issues, we are less likely to become 'triggered' by others at work. Whilst this might make sense at a logical level, this is often very difficult to do because past hurts run deep. After delivering a masterclass for a particularly challenging group of CEOs, one of them asked me to help him. I could feel his anger just by talking to him and he had gone through a pretty awful time in his life. As a child he felt lonely and isolated, believing his parents hated him, then his marriage to an alcoholic proved to be a disaster and ended in a bitter divorce. He then discovered scarring on his lungs and was full of worry about dying too early and not being able to bring up his children. At work he was a successful and driven man, yet he bullied his staff who were all terrified of him. He had become the bullying man that he resented in his father and was full of bitter recriminations. I remember reading a wonderful quotation by Gandhi who spoke about *the vessel that holds the poison is damaged most*. This man's anger and bitterness towards his father were all consuming and he was completely unaware of his own anger because of his seething resentment. It was only when I pointed out that as a father to his own kids he had become the complete opposite of his father. When he saw that his own experience of bad parenting had created the good parent he had become to his own children, he was able to see the 'gift' from his own father. At the moment of understanding he was able to let go of his anger and transcend to a place of peace and acceptance. It was his own experience of feeling unloved by his father that created his loyal and loving attitude with his own children. If you are committed to developing more of your authentic charisma, then you may need to explore the impact that your past has on your current experience of life. The leader you are today has been crafted from the programming received from your parents or the people who brought you up. The purpose of examining your parental relationship is to understand and come to terms with aspects of their behaviour through eyes of compassion. Your parents did the best they could with you; sometimes they may have got it wrong and sometimes they may have got it gloriously right. To understand the behaviours of parents, it can help to imagine what their own childhoods must have been like. What we perceive as acceptable through the eyes of an adult can be viewed as deeply traumatic through the eyes of a six-year-old child. One of the exercises I designed to help build self-worth involves a gift box. The idea is to view yourself through many different perceptual positions so you notice different aspects of your character. Part of the exercise requires identifying the positive gifts that you gained from your parents. When I first ran this exercise I was immediately challenged by a young woman whose father had left when she was four. She still felt anger towards him and told me that she received zero positive gifts from her father. I asked her how this had impacted upon her in a positive way and she replied that she learned to be independent and strong. These were the gifts from her father. I have worked with many people who grew up in an environment where their parents didn't show them much affection. At some level this left a mark and they became loving and affectionate parents to their own children. When you review your own parents with this objective in your mind and with a genuine and compassionate intention to understand, then you may notice you are able to access a deep sense of peace.

Select and play a piece of baroque music (various studies have found that baroque stimulates concentration and improves focus). Try 'Autumn Concerto' from Vivaldi's 'The Four Seasons' or Suite No 2 from Handel's 'Water Music'. Then, create two columns on a piece of paper and on the left hand side complete the sentence 'I lack charisma because…' Then, on the right hand side complete the sentence 'I am charismatic because…' Notice which column is longer. Then take each reason from the left hand column and rewrite it in the past tense. For example, 'I used to believe that I lacked charisma because [insert your reason] and now I realise that my past is just a story and I am charismatic when I am true to who I am at my core.' The process of writing your limiting beliefs in the past tense enables you to create an emotional detachment and neutralises any attached negative emotions.

Chapter 12

An audience with charisma

H istory is packed with charismatic leaders that have shaped and influenced the world we now live in. Can you imagine what insights might be gathered from a conversation with these leaders? Sociologist and distinguished professor, Edward Shils believed that a charismatic leader appears to be connected to the transcendental and superior powers of the universe. Quantum physics has established that, at the tiniest subatomic level, strands of pulsating energy connect everything into a unified field, could it be possible that the collective wisdom of charismatic leaders past and present can be shared and harnessed by everyone? My initial reaction to this theory was 'this is weird' until I had an experience that was destined to shake up my own beliefs and change the way I viewed flashes of inspiration and creative thinking.

Infinite intelligence

The late Napoleon Hill is widely considered to be one of the great writers on success. His most famous work, *Think and Grow Rich* (1937), is to this day one of the bestselling books of all time. Hill's 'secret of achievement' is widely considered to be the inspiration behind *The Secret*, Rhonda Byrne's (2006) bestselling book on the 'law of attraction' – based on the principle that what we think about we attract into our lives. Hill interviewed over 500 of the most successful people in the United States and included some exceptional thought leaders of their time: Thomas Edison, inventor of the light bulb, the motion picture camera and movie projector; Alexander Graham Bell, the inventor of the telephone; and Dr Elmer Gates who is renowned for his expertise in the use and manipulation of sound waves and electricity. It was working with these esteemed scientists that Hill observed that the human brain works in the same way as radio broadcasting because it is capable of picking up vibrations of thought that are being released by other brains. Along with Thomas Edison, Alexander Graham Bell and Elmer Gates, Hill developed a fascinating theory to explain that intuition, gut feelings, instincts and first impressions are all ideas that come from an 'infinite intelligence'. This is similar to what quantum physicists refer to as 'the field'. If Hill's theory is correct then you can, through your intuition, tap into the wisdom of charismatic leaders from the past. Hill's 13th step in his book, *Think and Grow Rich*, is referred to as 'the sixth sense: the door to the temple of wisdom'. He claims he was guided by ascended masters from a school of wisdom on the astral plane. Every evening he would set his intention to communicate with nine famous men from the past whom he had admired greatly. Hill visualised these nine impressive men, Emerson, Paine, Edison, Darwin, Lincoln, Burbank, Napoleon, Ford and Carnegie, sitting around a conference table where he would chair meetings to help his own development. Hill *never* claimed that he was channelling these men's wisdom yet he describes having flashes of insight and intuitive hunches that appeared to come from nowhere. Hill's book guided me to look at possibilities beyond my own belief system. I began thinking about which charismatic people from history I would invite to my theoretical conference table. What questions would I ask them? What wisdom would they share that could help people to become more charismatic? One rainy Sunday afternoon towards the end of summer 2013 I received a strong intuitive hunch about an idea that was so crazy, I instantly knew I was going to do it!

Replicating Hill's experiment

My vision was to hold a board meeting with 13 people whom I trusted and who in my opinion were highly intuitive and comfortable with exploring the unusual. Each person was asked to invite a charismatic guest with the proviso that their guest needed to be deceased. It was important that they selected and subsequently researched a charismatic leader with whom they felt a connection. Then, for 13 consecutive days, just before going to sleep, individuals would visualise asking their guest to attend this board meeting. The number 13 felt significant because the experiment related to Hill's *13th* step. I chose 26 October because it was the date in 1883 when Napoleon Hill was born. This would be 130 years exactly from the day Hill was born and I liked the synchronicity of *giving birth* to an idea that had been inspired by Hill on his birthday.

The event was chaired by a dear friend of mine, Paul Wayman, a gifted and trustworthy psychic medium. Paul's role was to induce a deep trance within the people attending and then invite their 'guests' to speak through that person and answer pre-prepared questions. This process is called channelling. I believe that everyone is capable of channelling a higher consciousness, whether it be their higher self, elevated soul, angel or otherworldly being. People can channel music, art, inventions, dance, knowledge and any form of expression. For example, Paul McCartney composed the melody of the song 'Yesterday' in a dream. He was so concerned that he had unconsciously plagiarised someone else's work that he waited a month before claiming that he had actually composed it. When channelling you can feel the change in the atmosphere as the presence of a higher energy. Many people tend to think that when channelling you effectively black out and the 'channelled guest' takes over but this happens in only the most extreme cases. Most channelling is where the 'guest' will influence the participant who may feel unsure whether it is their 'guest' speaking through them, or they are speaking as their own self. Both channelling methods are claimed to create 'inspired responses', so I was curious as to what would happen and whether we could generate or receive interesting answers. Napoleon Hill never claimed to be channelling because it would have ruined his reputation in the 1930s. But he did observe and record a direct correlation with extraordinary sparks of inspiration whenever he held one of his imaginary 'board meetings'. Because channelling is a controversial area, particularly for the world of business, I decided to invite Paul Matthews, HR expert, consultant on performance, capability and informal learning to witness the meeting. I requested he take photographs and give feedback of what he observed. Paul is a logical and methodical man with a highly developed intuitive side. He was neither a believer nor non-believer in channelling so would provide me with an objective perspective. He is completely honest and has high levels of integrity so I was thrilled he agreed to perform this role for me.

What questions to ask?

I run masterclasses with CEO groups and I asked some of the more 'open-minded' ones to contribute questions for the 'guests'. They were asked to respond to the question: 'If you could ask the most charismatic leaders of all time a question, what would you ask?' Each question received was typed onto a card and selected at random by Paul Wayman during the meeting. I felt that 'guests' might somehow influence the questions selected.

The invited guests

Because the idea for this meeting had been inspired by Napoleon Hill, I had a strong instinct that Mr Hill had chosen me. I felt a familiarity with many of his views that I gathered from my research. The rest of the guest list was impressive, eclectic and exciting.

- Martin Luther King
- Carl Gustav Jung
- Princess Diana
- Eleanor Roosevelt
- Winston Churchill
- Nikola Tesla
- Rangjung Rigpe Dorje, the 16th Karmapa
- Leonardo Da Vinci
- Neferneferuaten Nefertiti
- Mahatma Gandhi 'Gandhiji'

This 'audience with charisma' was recorded and transcribed afterwards. I have detailed extracts from this meeting later in Appendix 2. The words are incredibly powerful and in places very moving. At the beginning of the day there was a sense of impending excitement and curiosity that felt very intense. As the day progressed we were guided into deeper and deeper levels of trance so that at the point when our 'guests' showed up it felt as if we were detached from our mind and body and simply observing an experience unfolding before us. Many of our voices changed octaves and our phrasing differed from the way we usually speak. One of the group, a well-read and very knowledgeable lady who typically talks freely and expansively, uttered few words whilst responding as the 16th Karmapa. Our guests used words that were not choices they would typically make and, according to our observer, our bodies appeared to morph into the posture of someone else. Recorded observations described that it was palpable when Eleanor Roosevelt was present within the host's body, as if she was either drifting in or out, and her language would shift and change again, and was really fascinating to watch. The female host who channelled Winston Churchill adopted a masculine posture of one leg stretched out and one shoe was kicked off. Photographs taken that day recorded a high number of 'orbs' that when magnified showed some interesting phenomena. One of the leading theories concerning what orbs are is that they are indicators of energy being transferred from a source to a spirit so they can manifest. According to the laws of physics, energy being transferred in this way would assume the shape of a sphere. The right-handed host for Leonardo da Vinci drew a portrait with his left hand that looked identical to Leonardo's self-portrait. Nefertiti drew hieroglyphics that appeared to relate to the responses she had given. Her host reported that she felt a huge weight on top of her head, like a headdress that was really heavy. It made her sit very still. During the deepest trance session, all the photographs taken during this period were out of focus and looked as if there was an ethereal image hovering over our own physical bodies. The room temperature kept fluctuating and everyone's breathing got significantly slower and deeper. When we came back from the very deep trance there was evident surprise at what had happened. Many of us burst into tears, feeling overwhelmed by the intensity of what we had just experienced. We sat for awhile in stunned silence as it was difficult to process just what had occurred. There was a feeling of wonderment and a desire to reconnect with each other as if we had been away somewhere.

Conclusions

Did we channel a charismatic leader that day or were our responses simply inspired because we all felt so deeply relaxed? Did we access the Akashic records – a compendium of mystical knowledge encoded on the astral plane? And if not where did we receive our inspiration from? Is it possible that the wealth of learning accumulated by our guests during their lives on earth can still be shared by those keen to listen and learn? Decide for yourself as you read the recorded words from that day that are included in Appendix 2. Whatever conclusions you reach, these extracts give you a glimpse into why these leaders were so charismatic. You feel their passion behind the written word, sense the importance of their vision and understand that whilst their 'journeys' were not always easy they demonstrated an unusual blend of resilience and compassion. The strong dogmatic and impatient style of Winston Churchill demonstrates why he was such a great leader. Insights gained from Princess Diana about Charles show the depth of her love for him. Tesla's inability to articulate his inventions in real life was manifested in this meeting. He simply drew a schematic plan of one of his inventions and preferred to distance himself by sitting on the floor throughout. The beauty of Carl Jung's views and beliefs were wrapped in an aura of sorrow as his tortuous relationship with sex and his own authenticity was openly shared. Martin Luther King's fervour for equality and opportunity for all resounded in the hearts of all those present and his paced oratories caused pulses to race in a quest to say 'yes Mr King, we want this too'. Gandhi's calm and strong words transcended decades as we connected to the peace and humility he held within his heart. The simple powerful words shared by the 16th Karmapa caused tears to course down our cheeks as the words, 'love, love, love, that is all there is', strengthened our own connection to the love we felt strongly in our hearts. Eleanor Roosevelt's spiritual awareness and the impact she quietly made on her husband's leadership caused me to wonder who was the real driving force and inspiration behind President Roosevelt in his time? Then reflecting upon the eager and flowing replies from Mr Hill, I began to appreciate that his adversity had taught him so much and that we both shared high levels of resilience despite feeling on the verge of giving up on many occasions. Our observer was impressed by the lucidity of what he heard because usually when people are in a trance they tend to mumble.

– CHARISMA ENHANCER –

Select a deceased charismatic leader you admire and feel some connection with. Take an hour to research a bit about them. Sit at a table with a blank piece of paper and a pen. Focus on your breathing and allow your thoughts to slow down and drift away. When you feel relaxed imagine you are in a meeting with your chosen leader. Ask them for their advice on a particular problem. As you start to receive thoughts just write them down and keep writing until your mind becomes still once more. Then, read back what you have written and notice whether or not it has given you a new perspective to your particular issue.

Charisma accesses a higher power

This remarkable experiment showed me that when you develop the relationship with your unconscious mind and you are feeling safe, calm and supported, you start to feel in a wonderful state of flow. You feel connected with yourself, to others and to nature. Your senses appear wakened from a deep nourishing sleep so that small details catch your attention. You feel connected rather than separate from others and you start feeling as one with nature. In this place ideas flow freely, inspiring visions, next steps and revolutionary thoughts that just feel right to you. When we let go of our minds and tune into what we feel in our bodies we access a greater feeling of humanness. When we tap into the subtle energies of this sense of flow we find it easier to connect to love, courage and compassion. I remember reading the prose poem 'Desiderata' written by Max Ehrmann in 1927 and the following lines really jumped out at me:

> You are a child of the universe, no less than the trees and the stars; you have a right to be here. And whether or not it is clear to you, no doubt the universe is unfolding as it should… with all its sham, drudgery, and broken dreams, it is still a beautiful world.

Charismatic to the core

To increase your charisma you don't need to learn anything new. You simply have to feel comfortable being you, connect with your emotions and find purpose and personal meaning in your everyday work. It takes real courage to remain fundamentally true to who we really are inside. Years of environmental conditioning often stops us from honouring our softer and, therefore, more vulnerable side. Once we start to honour our true self we experience a feeling of euphoria at the sheer sensation of being alive. Charisma is our birthright, it is a natural state that is within all of us, including you, just waiting to be awakened.

As I reflect on some of the turbulent events from my youth, I see that every difficulty gave me the opportunity to experience a new facet of my character. Every challenge successfully overcome enabled me to experience a higher, better version of myself. To learn patience one needs to experience impatience. To learn acceptance one needs to let go of judgement and criticism. To connect and listen to your core self requires courage to let go of your protective walls, leaving you feeling vulnerable. Yet only when you are prepared to do this will you become ideally placed to access your natural and unique charisma. This letting go can often take a lifetime to achieve because it feels scary. You can't force charisma, you can't fake charisma. You simply have to allow it. In my view, the legacy of a truly charismatic leader is that when they look back over their life, they realise that their life was never about them. Their life's success is measured by how many people's lives they have positively touched and enhanced along the way. When we intuitively sense that an individual genuinely has our best interests at heart we follow them with unbridled loyalty, unwavering support and with complete trust that they will keep us safe. When you are brave enough to live in your truth you carve out paths for others to do so as well. My greatest wish for you is that you find the courage to let go of anything that stops you from being your true authentic self. Because when you are being you and you love what you are doing, you shine – and that is charisma.

Appendix 1

Exercises to enhance charisma

I have compiled a number of exercises designed to develop each of the five pillars of charisma: sensory awareness, self-esteem, compelling vision, driving force and balanced energy. These have been adapted from the exercises used during my charisma masterclasses that I have been teaching since 2008.

Readiness for change

Exercise objective: highlights how ready you are to make changes to your life and your charisma.

Identify an issue in your life that is preventing you from feeling more grounded in your life.

Now, complete your answers to these questions then assess whether your readiness to embark upon making changes has increased:

- What issues are you experiencing in your life right now that you'd rather not have?
- Which of these issues is causing you the biggest problem?
- Why is this issue a problem?
- What is likely to happen in the next year if you don't address this issue?
- Who else is your issue affecting?
- When you think about this issue, how does it make you feel?
- What have you done previously to resolve this issue?
- How committed are you to resolving this issue?
- What benefits do you gain from resolving this issue?
- When did you decide to create this issue?
- If you saw this issue as feedback from your unconscious mind, what could this issue be telling you?
- In what other areas of your life are you experiencing a similar issue?
- What recurring patterns are linked to this issue?
- What's this issue an example of?
- What emotional state relating to this issue are you experiencing most regularly?
- When you think about someone you really love, whereabouts in your body do you feel love?
- When you think about your issue, how do you feel?
- How often do you listen to and trust your intuition?

- How often, in a business context, do you express how you feel?
- What level of sensitivity do you have towards others?
- How much do other people affect your energy?
- Have you experienced major trauma in your past that still causes discomfort?
- How ready do you feel about letting your wall down?
- How confident do you feel that you have the resources you need to resolve your issues?
- What support is in place for you at this time?
- How have you dealt with intense emotions in the past?
- What's the worst that could happen as a result of committing to change?
- What's the best that could happen as a result of making this change?
- What do you need to believe that will enable you to get the most benefit from this change?
- What are the advantages you gain from this issue?
- What purpose does this issue serve?
- How does this issue protect you?
- What would you lose if you didn't have this issue?
- Who else do you know that has a similar issue to yours?
- How easy is it for you to resolve this issue?
- What is it about this issue that you have never told anyone?
- What are you pretending not to know by having this issue?
- Ask your heart, when did you decide to create this issue and for what purpose?
- Ask your unconscious mind if there is anything that your unconscious mind wants you to pay attention to such that if you were to pay attention to it the issue would disappear?
- Ask your unconscious mind is there anything that your unconscious mind wants you to know which will have the issue disappear?

Listening to your body

Exercise objective: helps you to notice how to experience emotions within your own body.

Every thought affects your emotions and creates a change within your energy. This in turn manifests itself within your physical body. When you are fully connected to your emotions you are able to feel a physical sensation within your body. Read out each of the seven statements below in turn and for each one notice the corresponding physical sensation.

Statements	Physical sensation
I am free	
I am scared	
I am good enough	
I am a failure	
I am loveable	
I am courageous	
I am compassionate	

As you begin to notice how your body reacts to different thoughts you can notice which thoughts empower or disempower how you feel. When you feel calm, relaxed and connected you are allowing your charisma to flow.

The metaphor reality method

Exercise objective: helps you to interpret metaphors to promote emotional healing.

How does a child get the attention of a busy adult? Usually, the child may call out or tug on the adult's sleeve. If the adult is engrossed in a conversation with someone else, the child may begin to whine and tug a little harder. If this doesn't work the child may start to wail and do naughty things, all because it is trying to get the adult's attention. Our unconscious mind is like our inner child, trying to get our attention when we are caught up in the 'busyness' of living our lives. Sometimes our unconscious mind gets our attention by creating something 'out of the ordinary' to ensure this message stands out from the crowds of thoughts milling around inside our heads. When we encounter something unusual in our day-to-day routine or something outside of the ordinary happens, we are being offered a metaphorical perspective. This new and unexpected perspective will provide us with an opportunity to reframe our thinking, change our perception and consequently change our emotional attachment linked to a stuck issue we are experiencing in our life. Developing your sensory awareness to the extent with which you notice these 'parallel ideas' will help you to explore an issue in different ways. I remember an occasion when three of my kitchen appliances, the dishwasher, oven and washing machine, had all broken down and each one had an electrical fault. My own lack of energy during a particularly busy period was hampering my ability to perform well at work. My broken kitchen appliances helped me to understand that if I didn't look after myself a bit better, I could end up having a breakdown. The essence of metaphor is understanding and experiencing one kind of thing in terms of another. I developed this process to enable you to uncover the meaning behind metaphors you encounter within your own life:

1. Be present/live in the *now*

   This allows you to act on the coincidences or metaphors that happen by operating with a more finely tuned emotional intelligence. Living consciously is choosing the situations you are in and the direction in which you are headed, living a life which you control. This means you are aware of your emotions as they arise, you notice your thoughts, you take care in what you are doing and you realise how you are affecting and influencing others. Living consciously is living in the now.

2. Acknowledge 'out of the usual' experiences

   Reflect on what unusual experiences have stood out to you recently. Spiritual guru, Deepak Chopra, states that 'Coincidences are not accidents but signals from the universe which can guide us towards our true destiny.' A person's name you have not heard for years, a chance encounter, a song or a phrase that you hear regularly. You may have experienced the anticipation of a call, moments before your phone rings, a chance meeting with an old friend who has just the advice you need, or a feeling of connection with a loved one miles away as they are going through a difficult time. Such experiences signal the hidden meanings in the universe, which call you to be as curious as detectives looking for clues that guide you to a more balanced and authentic way of living.

3. Capture initial response from your intuition

   Intuition is knowing something without being able to explain how you came to that conclusion rationally. It's that mysterious gut feeling or instinct that often turns out to be right, in retrospect. Therefore, as you think about your unusual experience, what thoughts spring to mind? What is this an example of? What does this represent to you? What could this mean in a different context? The more you listen to your instincts, the more readily you can trust them.

4. Identify reframed thought patterns

   Identify all the potential messages contained within your metaphor. This is a time to get down everything in your head onto paper or onscreen without any logical evaluation. Aim to identify at least three to five different meanings. You may find it helpful to take different aspects of your metaphor and identify different meanings for each aspect. You know when you have identified the correct meaning because you will feel a physical reaction within your body. So for each possible interpretation, notice your body's reaction.

5. Identify the message in the metaphor

   As you reflect on the message contained within this metaphor, ask yourself the question, 'What is the meaning of this message that just by knowing it will create a positive feeling of empowerment and understanding?'

Building self-worth

Exercise objective: helps you to appreciate more of your positive attributes to increase self-confidence.

Every word, image and emotion that you are exposed to over a period of time will either lower or develop your feeling of self-worth. Self-esteem flourishes in a positive environment. When you acknowledge and recognise qualities about yourself that you like then this strengthens your self-worth. Because you live with yourself your perception of you is subjective and may not be a particularly 'nourishing' perspective. This exercise expands your perception of you to enable you to notice attributes about yourself that have previously been unnoticed. Create a pile of rectangles made from paper about the size of an average business card. You'll need 25. Then, as you respond to these questions write each attribute/quality onto a separate rectangle:

- What three qualities do you admire most about yourself?
- Think of someone who really loves you. What three qualities do you believe that they love most about you?
- Think about a colleague at work who respects you. What three qualities do they respect about you most?
- Identify ten people in your life (from any context) who are important to you. For each person, identify the quality you believe they find most attractive in you.
- Think of a time in your past when you felt really good about yourself. Identify three qualities you possessed in this situation.
- Imagine a time in your future when you have accomplished everything you wanted to in your life. Describe three emotions you will probably feel.

Study your collection of positive qualities and select approximately seven qualities that feel important to you. Stand or sit in front of a mirror and prefix what you have written on each card with the words 'I am'. Lightly 'thump' your thymus gland that lies in the middle of your chest at the same time as you say each statement. Tapping your thymus will neutralise negative energy and imprint what you are saying at a deeper level. Keep your cards and review them whenever you lack confidence in yourself.

Letter to younger self

Exercise objective: helps to build understanding, self-acceptance and appreciation of yourself.

When you react to a situation that appears to be out of proportion to what is actually happening, then your younger self is probably 'loading your emotional deck' because of situations you experienced in your past. This may indicate that it's not your issue right now, it's an issue held by your younger self. Regardless of what makes sense to you as an adult, if it does not make sense to the younger you, then you will continue to become triggered by past events. Take a moment to reflect on you as a teenager. Knowing what you know now, what advice would you give to your teenage self? Write a letter of advice to your teenage self. You may find it's a very cathartic exercise for you both! Here is an edited version of my own letter to stimulate your creative juices.

Dear Nicola

You are going to experience life as a roller coaster rather than a roundabout. One thing I can promise you is that your life is never boring. Enjoy the exhilaration of the highs and remember that the lows give you a context for just how high you can fly. Embrace your emotions; they are powerful guides that shine light on whether your life is heading in the right direction.

There will be a time when your brother stops teasing you and your sister will always be a bigger man magnet than you. Despite what *Jackie* magazine says you can't 'train a boy to be a better boyfriend' – in fact you can't change other people only yourself. This is a lesson that you'll need to keep learning, because you'll discover that marriage is 'not 'til death do us part'. Never betray who you are, what you stand for and what is really important to you – people pleasing is not a selfless act. It causes more pain in the long term. View yourself as equally important as everyone else.

You can only wear one pair of shoes at a time and there will come a point when you'll choose comfort over style. Short skirts and low cut tops are not a good look for you and using household bleach on your hair will make it fall out. Do not put PVC into the tumble dryer – and remember that washing black and white together gives you lots of shades of grey.

Diets and crash diets make you fat. Throwing up after every meal is not cool. Healthy eating is not boring it is essential for your physical and emotional well-being. The next time you look critically at your body, despising the bits that are too large or wishing you were model thin, remember that it's the home that your soul has chosen to live in for as long as it feels welcome. Love and accept every part of yourself – you are exquisitely perfect in your unique imperfection. You are a much nicer person when you accept that being you is enough.

Remember to blow out the candles when you leave the house.

One day you'll have a daughter of your own. You adore her and feel so very proud of the woman she becomes. She teaches you how to love unconditionally.

Choose to do work that you love. Playing it safe will suffocate your soul. Only when you dare to take risks do you honour your infinite potential as this is the only way that you grow. You will experience quite a bit of fear in the next few years. What happens will define your character and you will understand why you have to go through this trauma in about 30 years' time. You are incredibly strong and you always get up every time you fall over. I am proud of you for possessing this quality.

Nicola, as you look up at the sky, if you can hear me, be true to yourself and trust your instincts. As you listen intently to the whispering trees, take a deep breath and prepare for an exciting 35-year journey knowing that I'm waiting to greet you when you arrive.

Learning from parents

Exercise objective: helps you to understand the positive gifts you have received from your parents to build acceptance and appreciation.

I once read a beautiful book by Mitch Albom – *The Five People You Meet in Heaven* – and this extract had a profound affect on me:

> All parents damage their children. It cannot be helped. Youth, like pristine glass, absorbs the prints of its handlers. Some parents smudge, others crack, a few shatter childhoods completely into jagged little pieces, beyond repair.

The impact that your parents have on your physical and emotional well-being has a profound effect on your self-worth. Experts acknowledge that what you experience during the first six years of your life will create a lasting impact throughout the rest of your life. This is because you are in a deep trance-like state absorbing everything like a porous sponge, including the values and beliefs of your parents. Little wonder that this parent-offspring relationship affects so many aspects of your personality including your charisma and personal presence. Limiting beliefs and values inherited from your parents may be sabotaging your happiness. Parental relationships can fuel intense emotional outbursts and are frequently 'blamed' for the mess or predicament you may find yourself in. If you view your parents as teachers, you can potentially learn from them in two ways. First, if they were role models of excellence and exuded positivity then your inner child will unconsciously seek to emulate them throughout your life. Alternatively, if your parents created trauma for you during your childhood, then you learn what you don't want to be and this has the potential to provide a catalyst for positive growth. For example, the child who felt unloved during their childhood often grows up to become a warm and physically demonstrative parent. A child who was abandoned by their father often grows up to be strong, independent and resilient.

Reflect and identify the positive qualities your parents have bestowed upon you, whether wittingly or unwittingly. If your parents did not bring you up then replace the word 'parents' with the names of the people who did.

Crafting a compelling vision

Exercise objective: helps you to create a compelling vision of a goal that is aligned with your core self.

A compelling vision creates a *purposeful striving* that utilises a process of *directed intention*. This creative power enables your thoughts to become things. This exercise is designed to connect you to the state, energy and flow accessed by charismatic people who possess a compelling vision.

- What attitudes and behaviours at work frustrate you most?
- If you had carte blanche to make one change in your business, what would it be and why?
- Who inspires you and why?
- What aspect of your career/business causes you to feel most alive?
- What special gifts do you possess, which if optimised could significantly benefit your company?
- Why do you believe this?
- What would you like to achieve within the context of your career/business within the next 12 months? *(Ensure this goal stretches you outside of your usual comfort zone.)*
- What specifically do you want to achieve?
- Why do you want to achieve this?
- Where are you now in relation to achieving this?

- How will you know when you have achieved it?
- Imagine achieving this, what will you see, hear and feel?
- What will this allow you to do?
- What do you need to do to achieve this?
- Will achieving this be OK for everyone else in your life?
- When you think about achieving this, what positive emotion are you feeling?
- Whereabouts in your body are you feeling what you feel?
- Can you intensify this feeling?
- As you think about this goal, how has the intensity of your desire changed?
- Why do you know with absolute certainty that you are going to achieve this?

Creating a colourful future

Exercise objective: helps you to shape your personal vision by working with your unconscious mind.

If you require some creative input regarding your personal vision then you can enlist the assistance of your unconscious mind by completing this exercise. You will need some paper plates (unwaxed), a variety of different food colourings and some paintbrushes. Find a piece of beautiful music that inspires and uplifts you.

Play your chosen music and take some deep breaths inhaling in through the nose and exhaling out through the mouth. Allow yourself to feel calm and relaxed.

Select a paper plate and using the food colourings paint one of your paper plates to reflect how you feel about your career/life right now.

Then, keep asking yourself the question 'What do I want?' and respond to yourself out loud.

Select another paper plate and, using the food colourings, paint one of your paper plates to reflect what you want to create in your future.

Then, compare your two painted plates and, using the following colour interpretation guide, notice the colours that are present in your second plate that are lacking in your first.

What conclusions can you draw from this process?

Colours	Meanings
Green	Healing, love, growth and emotional connectivity
Blue	Communication. A desire to express how you really feel
Red	Physicality, feeling grounded, action, ambition and determination
Yellow	Optimism, enthusiasm, intellect and positivity
Pink	Unconditional love, nurturing and support
Orange	Creativity, social connection and sexuality
Purple	Spirituality, perception and intuition
White	Purity, innocence, wholeness and completion
Black	Hidden, secretive, the unknown and blockages

Activating your driving force

Exercise objective: helps you to understand what drives you to ensure you make choices that are aligned with your career values.

Our values drive our behaviour which is why they have such a big impact on motivation and inner drive. Our values are unique to us and we have different values for different aspects of our life. To better understand what values are, it can help to appreciate what they are not. Things such as money and holidays are not values. If you believe that money is important to you in your career, ask yourself what money represents to you, such as success, independence or security – all of which are values. It also helps to review Maslow's hierarchy of needs in the knowledge that these are needs and are different to values. Values guide our needs, wants and goals and influence our daily decisions. A need is a necessity or essential items required for living our life, such as shelter, food and water. When you are doing something you love, you trigger your inner motivation and this natural drive energises your performance. When you are doing a job that does not satisfy your most important values then you will feel frustrated, drained and unfulfilled. Elicit your career values by asking yourself questions such as:

- 'What's important to me in my career?'
- 'What else is important to me?'
- 'When did I feel totally motivated in my career?'
- 'What was I feeling?'

Your aim is to find a minimum of eight values. Write each one on a separate piece of paper. Then, place your values in order of importance to you so your most important value is at the top. Take your time so you feel confident that you have correctly placed your values in their correct priority order. Reflect on how well your current job role is satisfying each of your career values using a scale of one to ten. Any value with a score of less than seven is cause for concern. You can then identify some specific actions around each of your poorly scoring values that will help you to increase your satisfaction level.

Developing a personal mantra

Exercise objective: helps you to create a powerful personal mantra to turbocharge your motivation.

Mantras are short phrases packed with energy and intention, specifically designed to generate powerful sound waves that promote healing, insight, creativity and emotional growth. You may have noticed well-known sportspeople muttering to themselves before or during an important event. Sports psychology is an emerging field of study on how our minds can affect physical and athletic performance. According to Peter Crocker, a sports psychologist and professor at the University of British Columbia, 'Elite athletes have been using psychological techniques for years… it used to be that something had to be wrong for an athlete to consult a sports psychologist, now they do it to gain an edge.' Repeating a mantra can activate your nervous system and instantly fire you up to ensure that you are in a peak and positive state.

Read through these statements and circle three that resonate with you. Then for each of your chosen statements underline the words in the statement that feel important to you. Make a list of all your underlined words and select three to five words that create an emotional reaction within you. Start writing your mantra using these words, ensuring your mantra starts with 'I am' or 'I have'. Finally, test your mantra by repeating it out loud and notice which version fires you up inside.

1. I want to work with people who are trustworthy, honest and reliable. People who seek to understand and give genuine, joyful praise.
2. I want to feel safe, secure and deeply appreciated.

3. I want to feel enthusiastic, alive and inspired.
4. I want to work with people who understand my need to create and manifest everything I desire most – abundance is my birthright.
5. I want my voice to be heard. I want to be really listened to. I want to work in an environment where I'm encouraged to think for myself. I want to work with people who operate with a hallmark of respect for everyone's thoughts, views and ideas.
6. I want to feel supremely confident in my ability to do my job well – knowing that I possess a unique brand of mastery that adds a 'special' ingredient to the work I choose to do.
7. I want to be recognised as a 'legend' rather than follow in the footsteps of others. I want to craft 'a way' from 'no way' because I am an adventurer who dares to risk losing to win.
8. I want to inspire and encourage others so they achieve more of their potential. To nurture and create an environment where people know that they matter and are supported in releasing their inner genius.
9. I want to cultivate ease, to be comfortable around the people I work with and be accepted and respected for who I am.
10. I want to contribute to a quest that is greater than my own personal success. I want to collaborate rather than compete, sharing the thrill of collective achievements.
11. I want to work in a place where I have the courage to say what I really feel and believe. An environment where a person's truth can be spoken and received with compassion and empathy.
12. I want to work in a spirit of equality where contentment and advancement are both similarly respected. Where everyone is given equal turns even in hierarchy, to help others do their own thinking.

Balancing your chakras

Exercise objective: helps to remove energetic and emotional blockages to stimulate the flow of energy around your body.

This process requires the use of a pendulum, a type of dowsing tool that amplifies the minute involuntary neuromuscular reactions of the human body to a stimulus, for example a question or command. You can buy a pendulum or make your own by attaching any heavy object onto a piece of string, ribbon or a chain. Holding the pendulum over each chakra in turn, you state your intention to *remove, take out and transmute any negative emotion or toxic energy from the chakra you are clearing*. Once your pendulum has stopped moving, you then state your intention to *send love and healing to the chakra you are balancing*. Generally your pendulum will rotate in an anti-clockwise direction when removing toxic emotions and rotate in a clockwise direction when sending in positive and healing energy. If working with your own chakras, place your hand palm down onto the chakra you are balancing, to reinforce your concentration. This is best achieved by sitting upright in a chair that supports your back.

Boosting energy quickly

Exercise objective: helps to turbocharge your energy for an immediate boost of physical and mental power.

This exercise gives you a rapid and powerful boost to your energy levels. I used it extensively when I used to coach people to break a thick piece of wood with their bare hands. By pumping up their energy, they automatically pumped up their confidence and were able to break the wood even though it was stronger than the bones in their hand.

- Stand with your feet shoulder width apart.
- Keep your knees soft and stretch yourself up to your full height.
- Raise your arms and clasp your hands above your head whilst inhaling.
- Then exhale sharply and use a sharp, strong pulling movement down towards your abdomen whilst keeping your hands grasped together.
- Repeat this process at a steady pace about ten times.
- You'll feel a sense of energy circulating around your body.
- If you feel light-headed, stop.

Triggering positivity

Exercise objective: helps you to instantly access a highly resourceful state of mind.

You already know that your thoughts and emotions change your physiology and any changes in any of these areas will change your energy. When I feel excited and passionate about something I raise my eyebrows, use more hand gestures and speak quickly. These movements have become physiological triggers – they automatically connect me to feelings of excitement and passion. I also say to myself in a 'Rocky' type way, 'I can do this – go get 'em Nikki.' Regardless of how I am feeling, when I use my physiological triggers with my positive self-talk, I feel a shift in my energy almost instantaneously.

- Identify a time when you felt powerful, confident and charismatic.
- Go back to that time, see what you saw, hear what you heard and feel what you felt.
- Imagine explaining why you feel so passionate to someone else.
- Notice what changes occur in your physiology – these are your triggers.
- Use these triggers and notice your energy increase.
- For additional power repeat your personal mantra with your physiological triggers.

If you are keen to benefit from more exercises, meditations, visualisations and processes that gently help you to increase your charisma then take a look at my 12-month audio programme, 'Activate Your Charisma', by visiting nikkijowen.com/activateyourcharisma

Appendix 2

Transcript from channelling event

These extracts are taken from recordings of the Channelling Deceased Charismatic Leaders Event on Saturday 26 October 2013. For the purpose of ease I have referred to Paul Wayman as 'Medium', and used the names of the guests that we were aiming to channel.

If you are interested in listening to the original audio recording of the main trance session please visit nikkijowen.com/channellingaudio

Medium: I would now like to address Napoleon Hill who is with us now and I would like to ask Mr Hill that maybe he could start this meeting by outlining what you would like to achieve. Mr Hill, please feel free to talk, if you wish.

Napoleon Hill: It's a good thing. We come together to learn, to expand and to share ideas from across the great divide. I welcome so many of our great minds here today. I see a world similar to the world I once knew. A world where men's minds were easy prey for the devil and these are challenging, tough times and I believe that every man has the key. Every man has a key and we can achieve so much and it is so easy to do. I am still learning. I am still keen to learn and I, yes, yes, thank you, and Mr Carnegie. He too is here with me and we are… we're laughing… it's a really good thing, we are doing.

Medium: Thank you for talking to the group. And I would now like to address all of the guests here with us now and I would like them to consider this next question. What is the greatest human virtue? Neferneferuaten Nefertiti can you please talk to the group?

Neferneferuaten Nefertiti: Just one word. It's love and it comes from our creator, the sun, Aten. Aten is the source of all life. Aten is the source of love. It is love.

Medium: Thank you. Would any of the other guests… Leonardo, would you like to speak?

Leonardo da Vinci: Love is important but the word that came to me was curiosity, above all things it's what sets us apart as humans. Curiosity… the first order stand.

Medium: Thank you Leonardo. I would now like to invite the 16th Karmapa to address the group, please?

The 16th Karmapa: Yes, both important but love needs wisdom or it is foolish.

Gandhiji: Love is if it's unextinguishable under any circumstances and therefore forgiveness is critical.

Medium: Thank you. I would now like to go to the next question and once again invite the guests to offer their wisdom, their opinions, their experiences. As I ask them, if you could teach each child in the world, one lesson, what would it be and why? And if you would like to answer, please raise your hand. Thank you. Napoleon?

Napoleon Hill: Please call me Mr Hill. To me the power of the mind is everything. We have a power that is beyond us as physical beings. We have a power that can touch and transform everything our heart desires and if we allow our mind to just open to that potential. That vast landscape of possibility, that immense pleasure of all that we want is there in each and every one of us and for the schools, for the education systems, for a child to learn that this is so from birth. Can you imagine what mankind could create with the wisdom and passion of that piece, that single piece of knowledge?

The 16th Karmapa: Mind is everything. The world of duality must be seen as illusory. Unity, we are all one.

Martin Luther King: If we believe, we can achieve. Through the thought process and constant focus anything is possible.

Eleanor Roosevelt: I believe, for sure, with love for sure but to teach, to play and enjoyment is crucial.

Winston Churchill: Never, never, never give up… to give up is to die.

Medium: And you illustrated that throughout your life. Thank you for sharing that. Dr Jung?

Carl Jung: The children bring the light. They bring the light into the world. And it is the light that needs to be encouraged not stamped on and it's important for us to learn through the eyes of the children before it is dark.

Gandhiji: Yes, all very important but remember the greatness of what you are will intimidate many people so humility and being not too big and not too proud is really important. People will listen.

Neferneferuaten Nefertiti: As all things are created so we are constantly creating and the greatest teaching and understanding is to consciously praise through love and with love.

Medium: Thank you. Now I would like to move on to the next question. And I would like to direct this question initially at Diana. During your life, how would you describe your relationship with yourself? If you feel comfortable, please speak.

Princess Diana: This is the question I was anticipating. I was hard on myself and I forgot that I was always connected to a source of all goodness and kindness that would have been more supportive of me had I remembered it. My frailties showed up in many ways and were perpetrated by others. And yet there is forgiveness in me I could not believe. How should I say this? It was difficult to understand the horrors and the way I was treated by those who I thought would have been more kind to me, knowing my position.

Medium: Thank you Diana for sharing that. I appreciate your insights. I would like to offer that question open to any of our other guests here today. During your life, how would you describe your relationship with yourself? If you would like to offer your views, please raise your hand. Thank you, Gandhiji.

Gandhiji: A continuous battle. A bigger battle inside than the battle is outside. Other people are easy but always to know the truth within yourself, never to block yourself out.

Napoleon Hill: Resilience can be a good thing. How can we learn resilience without the dark, without the bleak, without the winters and it's at those moments when we are absolutely at a depth when there is hunger in our bellies and it's dark and it's a scary, scary place. It's at those moments when we choose to face ourselves and at that point we can really know who we are destined to become.

Leonardo da Vinci: As I think of this question, there are tears in my eyes now. I spent my life seeking to understand anatomy, mechanics and now I understand that for a man to fly, it has nothing to do with this physical show. It's about believing, just believing you can.

Eleanor Roosevelt: Oh yes. I think that our critics are actually very useful, looking at ourselves from within and from that, I personally, found the strength to fly, indeed, to fly.

Carl Jung: I sought in my life to go to the deepest parts. I needed to separate before I could integrate. I needed to see my shadow in order to be whole.

Martin Luther King: Well relationship is about expansion. Every man and woman should be able to express through their similarities. No one should be suppressed or oppressed and we should be able to demonstrate this message with clear and non-violent signals.

The 16th Karmapa: My training from a young child was that self is a condition of the grasping ego mind and to become enlightened, one only has to realise this truly and fully. Self is a construct and that we are all just one universal mind. To realise the 'I' is a condition, a mental thing of the ego… that there is no 'I'… the sooner we realise the actual oneness of Mind with a capital 'M' and get beyond ego grasping, the better for all sentient beings.

Napoleon Hill: The ego… the devil. It's the devil's work. You call it ego, I call it the devil. And it's all about weakness, weakening of the mind and the weakening of the mind, weakens the spirit, weakens the soul, weakens the essence of who we are. And yet for every weakness, for every ego, for every devil, there is its counter opposite.

Medium: Thank you Mr Hill. I'd now like to direct this next question to Mr Churchill and ask who or what was the biggest influence on your life and why? Please step forward and speak if you wish to do so.

Winston Churchill: I was the biggest influence. I called for my mother and she didn't come. It had to be me. That's made me the man I am today.

Martin Luther King: God was undoubtedly the biggest influence on my life. Through his teachings I understood that love was an essential for our being. My father and grandfather were great men. I followed in their footsteps and became a Pastor. Because God was the one with the greatest message for all of us. That's why I reverently believed in non-violence. Through non-violence and turning the other cheek, I was able to demonstrate and deliver my message clearly.

Princess Diana: There have been many influences… key people… influences in my life. And yet I think the biggest was my friend and my husband Charles. He is a very kind and generous man and much maligned. We have so many similarities and I saw how he handled them with his graceful ease and he was a very big influence and role model. I am proud that he is the father of my children. There was a teacher who influenced me a great deal as a child. The only person I could go and speak to in my childish and unconfident like way. That was never betrayed by her and for that I am very grateful.

Medium: That's wonderful you feel at peace with that. Thank you Diana. And I would also like to ask that question to Mr Tesla. And you may speak, you may write or draw but who or what was the biggest influence on your life? [No response from Nikola Tesla.] Thank you. And now moving forward, I would like to get the attention of our guests once again and ask, in their opinion and their experience, what is possible for a human being. Miss Ellie, would you like to offer your thoughts on that?

Eleanor Roosevelt: Everything is possible. You just have to believe it is.

Medium: Did you always believe that yourself, Miss Ellie?

Eleanor Roosevelt: Fifteen I would say. Then I kind of really understood it more… I was on my own so… with my own thoughts. My parents died and my father with his weaknesses and then so much pressure. It's so easy to just go within and hide and just let it all wash over you and if you start seeing what you can achieve, just with a thought.

Medium: You must have a great strength of will. Thank you for sharing that. And I would like to address that question to the 16th Karmapa. What is possible for a human being?

The 16th Karmapa: When a human being is enlightened, everything. Everything, their consciousness is the size of the cosmos or as small as a pinhead.

Medium: And how do you feel if I may ask, when you see human beings not reaching their potential?

The 16th Karmapa: They have more chances, more lives.

Martin Luther King: I would certainly like to add my humble opinion. Anything is possible through belief, through focus, through love. Anything is possible. If we allow our spirit to be crushed, then nothing is possible but as long as we are open to hearing the Father, everything and anything is possible.

Eleanor Roosevelt: May I just add. This has to start at ground roots level with our children. We can start from here and filter through but it needs to start here and teach them rather than through fear.

Leonardo da Vinci: More profoundly, I think it starts with language with the definitive article 'a', a human being, his ego, the human being, the one. And when we realise that, everything is in our grasp.

Neferneferuaten Nefertiti: All things are possible. We are all one, it's simply a case of choosing to demonstrate that fact.

Medium: Thank you for your words of wisdom. And I would now like to ask Gandhiji. As a leader, what are you most proud of?

Gandhiji: For myself, nothing, there is more I could have done. For others, it's taking things forward, moving things forward. In gatherings like this where we realise that actually the torture of humanity is being on the earth. Most proud of… all those who make the effort to put ego aside, moving forward.

Napoleon Hill: These are words of so much wisdom. They hold the power to transform the hearts and minds of everyone and I am truly humbled in the presence of so many great minds. I am not usually a man lost for words yet my heart absolutely flies and I bow to the greatness of the presence.

Medium: Can I also follow up that question Mr Hill, with another? What do you consider to be the secret of your success?

Napoleon Hill: Desire. Oh, when I want something, I absolutely make it happen. And what is it with the apathy of people today that they put their desires to one side. They get lost in the fog of living their lives with such drab monotony. When did we stop listening to what it is we really want? Desire is the thing that makes man a fortune. Desire that sets him on his path. Desire is, it is the start, it is the first step, it is the point where we make a commitment to ourselves because we say this is what I want.

Medium: Mr Hill, your desire shines through. Thank you for your words. Dr Jung when you look back on your life, what would you have done differently?

Carl Jung: I have pondered this. What I would have done differently? I would have spoken out more freely, I would have rejected the ideas that were not true to me. I had many opportunities, early in my career, to follow the path of my soul. I was drawn away by many avenues that took me to places that did not serve my higher purpose. I would have wished for more time to the second part of my life. I descended into the abyss. I lost my mind and it was through losing my mind that I connected and I pursued as Mr Hill said, my desire.

Medium: And do you regret that Dr Jung?

Carl Jung: The path of the soul is a complex one. We come into these lives in ways that make us forget. It takes a lifetime to incarnate and I appreciate that. I was in such a hurry to taste the world and I lost myself in the world. And it was through madness and finding my way back out of the abyss, that I realigned myself and found my life.

Medium: I hope you are at peace with that now Dr Jung, thank you. And I would like now to ask Neferneferuaten Nefertiti what constitutes your uniqueness. Can you please define that?

Neferneferuaten Nefertiti: We are all one. Simply the choice and the determination to follow the truth as we understand it at any given time. And I recognise the truth, others recognise the truth and we should never allow ourselves to be defined by race, or gender or economics. Nor make our beliefs so formalised that we gather so many followers and if I were to answer the previous question, that would be what I would change.

Princess Diana: I would define my uniqueness from the greatness of my heart. I would define my uniqueness now and it is something I would share with others. That to remember that you are God, remember that you are whole, remember that you have a gift and a unique gift to offer that only you can, and to have the determination, wisdom and the collective group of followers and supporters who will help you on your path to your destiny.

Medium: Thank you Diana. And now I would like to ask Leonardo. How would you describe your most positive attribute?

Leonardo da Vinci: In the same way that I answered the previous question and I would simply say that mostly I was just very good at getting out of my own way. I just got out of the way and let God's work, work through me.

Medium: At what point in your life did you realise that you were going to do something remarkable? Dr King would you like to answer that?

Martin Luther King: This is very easy. In answer to the question, we are all remarkable… it is just whether we choose to show how remarkable we really are and that takes courage that's all. But in the eyes of the Creator we are all remarkable.

Winston Churchill: I was sent to Harrow as a young boy and I found that when I spoke, people listened. When I spoke louder, people followed and I knew I would be a great leader from then and I was a great leader.

Napoleon Hill: I felt ordinary, ordinary really, like any other man. And I met, at the age of 23, a man who inspired me to look for the way that any ordinary man could make himself set apart and become extraordinary. And I believe it is not who we define ourselves as, it is what mark we make on the world. And that determines how remarkable our legacy will become.

Neferneferuaten Nefertiti: There is no one any greater or any lesser than anyone else and there just came a point in my life when I realised because I was willing to stand up and speak the truth, my truth as I knew it and understood it, at any given time… it created an impact. That was not the intention, it was simply the effect.

Leonardo da Vinci: Native American indigenous people name their children after the first unusual thing they see... it's a metaphor. There was a kite that hovered over my crib so close to my face that its tail feathers touched it. I always saw this as the moment and it's just come to me now that, it's seeing the elements, seeing the metaphors and understanding them. That's what it's about.

The 16th Karmapa: Karmapas 1 to 15 are in me and I am in the 17th but not I, my consciousness, their consciousness, our consciousness.

Carl Jung: I knew as a young boy, the path I was to take, entered through the world of dreams and this was the thread that carried me through. This is the thread that had the connection to a greater power. This is the thread that took me through the illusions and I knew with perseverance... I was blessed with perseverance... the secrets, the mysteries would unfold beneath my feet by treading this path and through the world of dreams.

Medium: Thank you Dr Jung. I would like to thank all of my guests for this first part, Mr Hill, Mr Tesla, Diana, Neferneferuaten Nefertiti, Miss Ellie, Mr Churchill, the 16th Karmapa, Gandhiji, Dr King, Dr Jung and Leonardo.

The following responses from the group of deceased charismatic leaders were obtained using an inspired writing technique that involved writing whilst in a deep trance-like state. Three questions were asked and the responses were interesting and in some cases unexpected.

Question one – Why are you here today?

Napoleon Hill: When I studied the legacy work, I recognised we are more than just mankind and we can access a knowledge of such resource, such wisdom that I knew in an instant, I was going to test it out at the point of my passing. And I have many times sought to influence the minds of others so they created an inspired thought and inspired feeling and that is my legacy to them.

Nikola Tesla: Curiosity, opportunity, future, vibration, frequency, universe, unity and free.

Princess Diana: I wanted to put my ideas across to you and share my wisdom with you. There was so much that was written about me that was true and so much that was false and created. I have so much love and pride in myself, I love life, love Charles… I love the people in my life… my children I worshipped… I am so proud of them. I am a grandmother in spirit. I visit my children and my grandchild every night. They are my deepest love and my most remembered and treasured contribution.

Neferneferuaten Nefertiti: I am here today as it is time again for a great shift to world truth. My life before as Neferneferuaten Nefertiti was about truth. We are now at another great step forward and I think that all now is in alignment.

Eleanor Roosevelt: The reason for my presence here today is to rejoin with formidable forces to strengthen a collective link, rearrange some misconceptions that may or may not have occurred during our lifetime. Make this a way of strengthening and bring forth the wisdom of old, our heads and sages to enlighten the lives of those on this earth plain.

Winston Churchill: I am here today because I have been called to do so. I have made mistakes and I have many successes which I would like to share. I recognise, I can still learn and there are a lot of things, I don't know about. I know how to win wars and battles but I don't know about all this other spiritual stuff. That doesn't win wars. People need to believe in me and what I stand for. People do believe. I enjoy being involved at the centre. It is right that I am here today. It's right that I'm here now.

The 16th Karmapa: Love, love, love altogether. Compassion for the world of sentient beings. Meditate on love, compassion, generosity, forgiveness.

Gandhiji: To help improve the world, to remove some of the barriers to ascension and lead this planet and go to the central plain. Ascending and leaving behind all the rubbish and evil. The light and darkness are two competitors for energy and for our energy. We must help people to learn to produce more positive light, to shine out and light up all the dark recesses of the world especially the corners of people's hearts so that love can live strongly there.

Martin Luther King: I feel my presence has been required because I still had questions to answer and opinions to give. I went too early before my job was complete but I am happy my messages were worked upon because the world has become more treacherous in many ways but maybe not as divided.

Carl Jung: To understand again the limitations that keep us from being able to be fully integrated and get all the information we so eagerly seek. The understanding that groups of people can show different colours and perspectives of life in all areas is infinite. Now is such an important time in history. I wish I had lived in my body and knew to see this place and how it feels in this new vibrational state.

Leonardo da Vinci: I am here today to share. I never shared. If I had, medical science could have been moved on hugely. I am here because I am curious about the world as it is now, inventions, the progress and the humanity.

Question two – What makes a leader truly charismatic?

Napoleon Hill: A man with great passion will enthuse the hearts of many. Great passion is magnetic. Great passion evokes men to reach out and embrace the stars. Great charismatic leaders can turn a simple pebble into a nugget of pure gold.

Nikola Tesla: Honesty, determination, heart, compassion, modest, understanding, patient and loving.

Princess Diana: Honesty, fun, truth and a love of connection. One who is with oneself with all the lumps and bumps this brings. A charismatic leader has humility and a desire to seek the best of a person and who connects at a soul or heart level. One who is willing to learn with spirit.

Neferneferuaten Nefertiti: Love and light, truth and beauty, courage expressed with courage and faith and commitment and always from love.

Eleanor Roosevelt: A charismatic leader is one not stuck in any of their own beliefs and knowledge but has the wisdom and strength to listen with very open ears and minds and to answer it with an undoubtable solution imparting compassion and true strength to all.

Winston Churchill: Belief in self, total resilience, strength and determination. Of course you have to be humble enough to recognise you do not always get it right but at least you believed at the time you were right. It was my best intention. Laughter and being able to engage with others also gets everything done.

The 16th Karmapa: Love plus wisdom and compassion and don't forget the laughter and enjoy.

Gandhiji: Someone who walks the talk, someone who does the right thing with integrity. Evil charisma can mislead those who are gullible but the truth always will prevail. Love, truth, wisdom and integrity will always dominate those who wish to humiliate, crush, control and dominate others, using their charisma. It's power versus force, it's God versus the devil in old speak.

Martin Luther King: Talking from the heart, we all hear messages from inside and it is our job to interpret these message and voices and deliver the message in a manner that can be understood by many. Having the presence and the power to be heard is a critical factor but also belief in the message you are delivering.

Carl Jung: This is a process of allowing all aspects to be integrated and expressed so that the unacceptable and acceptable can join to form in a greater vessel which can hold the enormous potentiality of the human spirit without judgement or censorship. An expression of life itself in its purest, unashamed form.

Leonardo da Vinci: A leader becomes truly charismatic when you know that they have a true heart and that their words and deeds are consistent. Charismatic leaders demand absolute confidence and maturity.

Question three – If there was one piece of advice for the benefit of mankind in the 21st century, what would it be?

Napoleon Hill: Use your mind, use your mind, use your mind, use your mind, use your mind, use your mind. This is a magical opportunity to raise the conscious awareness to many leaders who are reliant on old-fashioned methods of shaping the success of their empires. We urge you to promote, to discuss, to talk about your work. We urge you to meet again and at the point of your collective readiness, all will be revealed.

Nikola Tesla: Live free! Expand to encompass all consciousness both present and past.

Princess Diana: To honour yourself, each other and to be grateful. In a larger sense to love the earth and the heavens as if it was your own self. To stop spoiling and maiming our children in the name of power. To stay, reconnect and recreate the specialness and enjoyment of our visits. To embrace and cherish the time… this is a connection not an exercise. We each love you and wish to share our wisdom.

Neferneferuaten Nefertiti: Let go of fear, let go of fear, all is love, let go of fear, all is well, all is love and all will return to love. Sharing wisdom and love. Connecting to source and remembering that we are all one. Demonstrating that we are all one and time and space do not exist.

Eleanor Roosevelt: Live your life, laugh at everything until you cry with joy or release the pain of whatever it is is holding you back in your goals or achieving your desire, never listen to criticism and take it on as your own. I suggest we meet at regular intervals and create a board of wisdom directors that the knowledge be transcribed for the growth and well-being of those on your planet. We are here to serve.

Winston Churchill: Be kinder to each other, war is not the answer. Be decisive, better to have got it wrong than never have made a decision. Be proud. We can learn from others. The group can be used at times of conflicts to help make joint decisions providing it was logical and not too much of the unknown. This is a reminder to keep special and knowledgeable people around you. You don't need to do it yourself.

The 16th Karmapa: Realise your unity, one Mind, one everything. Know it, realise it, live it. Create more groups, spread the ideas.

Gandhiji: Speak up, or become leaders. Do not hesitate, take right action, do not think. Take the first step with your message, let other wise people come with you until the voice becomes a clamour and then everything will overcome negative messages. Speak up against evil and stupidity. To help develop messages that will move humanity along. So we must connect with the collective wisdom and understanding at the highest level and then pace them and lead them. We must never force those who wish to follow shallow lives with trivial distractions but we must help people be what they can be.

Martin Luther King: Always be true to yourself and your conviction. This is critical. If you are not true to yourself with conviction, you cannot deliver a believable message. We must use the energy to draw information from past great minds so we can continue to shape our future. Knowledge and wisdom are only powerful when used effectively.

Carl Jung: To see through the veils, the charlatans and the deceivers. Trust the innate wisdom that constantly shows its face in all the things around. The whispers and the omens; the symbols and the signs that constantly direct your path and support your journey to wholeness. This has been a good start and has taken much to pass through to be expressed. Each time will be easier and it is important to use this forum to gain a greater level of information and guidance to come through at this great time of need on this plane.

Leonardo da Vinci: Water is the key, water is the key to life on earth, all the energy and power needed is within the ebb and flow of the oceans and the rivers. Each of us should understand that the link has been established and the curtain lifted. We are one. We all have access to the library and the knowledge. Ask and it is given.

This ends the transcript from the trance session.

The experience was difficult to understand and process and I thought it would be interesting to include the final thoughts of the people involved. Their feedback was also recorded on the day.

Nikki Owen – Napoleon Hill: I feel emotional. This has been an incredible experience. Really profound. The love in the room was overwhelming.

Anthony Edwards – Nikola Tesla: I feel privileged because I feel like I've been lucky enough to get a few useful words out of people who I may not have ever heard from otherwise. Pretty cool.

Sue Bottomley – Princess Diana: I feel really grateful and very privileged. I feel quite humbled by the integrity and the honesty in the room. That's very very special.

Jessica Richards – Neferneferuaten Nefertiti: I was absolutely fascinated to hear what other guests had to say as well. I can't wait to read the transcripts back. I can't remember why I said most of it… but I actually can remember what some of the other guests said. I even remember putting my hand up and having no idea what was going to be said.

Suz Jeffery – Eleanor Roosevelt: I was very grateful to have the opportunity to do this. Those amazing… people… physical embodiments… and the ones that came in through us… for us all collectively to share.

Angela Tickner – Winston Churchill: I definitely feel I chose the right person for all of the right reasons and it feels that each person that everybody chose was the right person for them. I am feeling really good that Mr Churchill chose me and I am privileged I chose him and part of me is a bit concerned because I don't really want to lose him now to be honest. I am not sure if it will come to that because I'd love to be able to call on him when I need him. Especially because of some of the words I got from him at the end.

Sue Skinner – the 16th Karmapa: An absolutely amazing day. When I was coming here this morning, I was thinking, have I had a bit of a nerve actually choosing to channel an enlightened being. And then I thought well actually, if he's enlightened, he won't mind in the least!

Richard Tickner – Gandhiji: In awe. Absolutely brilliant. I have to say as we were going through the main part, about half way through, something the 16th Karmapa said sparked up something within and I was just completely flooded with the most brilliant purple light.

Kevin Dwyer – Martin Luther King: I am not usually a man of few words, I have usually got plenty to say. But I would like to just summarise the whole experience for me in four words: grateful, profound, surreal and drained. It's been remarkable, it really has. Thank you.

Corah Clark – Carl Jung: I didn't have any notion of how this was going to be and it's the first time I've been in anything like this. I was just wanting to be clear and so most of the time I was focusing on just trying to be receptive instead of worrying about: Is this really happening, is it not? It felt so crowded in here at one point. I am a believer… do you know what I mean… because of what I felt. If I had been outside of it, looking at me, I'd be just wondering… I don't know about that… but I was shaking after, it took me a long time to get back to feel myself, my fingers… everything. So that was interesting, I've not had that before.

Mark Wharton – Leonardo da Vinci: As an exercise in creative thinking, if you were to publish a lot of those things that were said today and put them on the internet, I think it would be hard to tell whether some of those quotes came from what happened today and what came from the real people. Certainly I was emotional, there was definitely tears coming out. It was very easy for me to feel that I was in the presence of something quite extraordinary so I loved it!

Key people, events and terms

Addezio, Mario. Barrister, called to the bar 1971.

Alessandra, Tony. American best-selling author, entrepreneur and motivational speaker.

Ali, Muhammad born Cassius Marcellus Clay, Jr. (b. 17 January 1942). American, former professional boxer.

Aljazeera televised first UK election debate (May 2010). With Nikki Owen, charisma and confidence expert.

American Rhetoric Top 100 Speeches. 'I have a Dream' delivered 28 August 1963 at the Lincoln Memorial, Washington DC, by Martin Luther King.

Angelou, Maya (1928–2014). An American author, poet, dancer, actress and singer. She received dozens of awards and more than 50 honorary degrees.

Audience with Charisma seminars at Shakespeare's Globe Theatre London from 2008 to 2012.

Behavioural Similarities Chart from 'Releasing your hidden charisma' by Nikki Owen 2008.

Bell, Alexander Graham, (1847–1922). Eminent Scottish born scientist, inventor, engineer and innovator who invented the first practical telephone.

Big Apple Experiment™ founded by Nikki Owen in 2010 to demonstrate the impact of directed intention on physical reality.

Blair, Tony (b. 6 May 1953). British Labour Party politician who served as the Prime Minister of the United Kingdom 1997–2007.

Bohr, Niels Henrik David (1885–1962). Danish physicist; Nobel Prize in Physics in 1922 for his contribution to understanding atomic structure and quantum theory.

Bottomley, Sue. Energy coach and teacher of mindfulness who chose to channel Princess Diana on 26 October 2013.

Branson, Sir Richard (b. 1950). Founder of Virgin Group.

British Society of Dowsers founded in 1933 by Colonel A.H. Bell.

Broadmoor Hospital. High security psychiatric hospital in Berkshire, England.

Brown, Elizabeth. A master dowser and a causative diagnostician who uses dowsing to identify the causes of emotional and physical illness. She was awarded the Bell Award by the British Society of Dowsers for achievement in notable written work and in 2014 she was awarded the Floyd Cup for outstanding contribution in the field of health dowsing.

Brown, Gordon. Prime Minister of the United Kingdom 2007–2010; Chancellor of the Exchequer 1997–2007.

Businessballs. Free online educational resource.

Byrne, Rhona. *The Secret*, published in 2006, was based on the law of attraction and was influenced by Wallace Wattles' 1910 book *The Science of Getting Rich*.

Cannon, Walter Bradford (1871–1945). American physiologist, professor and chairman of the Department of Physiology at Harvard Medical School. Coined the term 'fight or flight response', written in his book *The Wisdom of the Body* first published in 1932.

Carney, Mark (b. 1965). Canadian central banker and Governor of the Bank of England.

Chapman, Alan. Owner of the free online educational resource Businessballs

Cheese, Peter. Joined the Chartered Institute of Personnel and Development (CIPD, the professional body for human resources and people development) as chief executive in July 2012 after 30 years of working at Accenture.

Cheng Yen (b. 11 May 1937). Taiwanese Buddhist nun, teacher and philanthropist who leads a worldwide social welfare movement with five million devotees.

Chopra, Deepak. An Indian-born American author and public speaker who is a western-trained doctor and an Ayurvedic practitioner. He is an alternative medicine advocate and a promoter of popular forms of spirituality.

Churchill, Winston (1874–1965). British Prime Minister from 1940 to 1945.

Clark, Corah (Ann Eaton). EFT and transpersonal therapist who chose to channel Carl Jung on 26 October 2013.

Clinton, Bill (b. 1946). 42nd President of the United States.

Conant, Vic. Chairman of the board of Nightingale-Conant Corporation. Contributed to the report 'The five most dangerous issues facing sales leaders today and how to guarantee a permanent improvement in sales results', which was based on a survey conducted with 2,663 organisations globally.

Craig, Gary (b. 1940). Founder of Emotional Freedom Techniques and a certified master for neurolinguistic programming. He is a Stanford engineering graduate and an ordained minister.

Crocker, Dr Peter. A professor in the School of Human Kinetics at the University of British Columbia. He was the director of the school from 1999 to 2004. His research focuses on stress and adaptation, with a particular interest in understanding health-related behaviour. *The World Sport Psychology Sourcebook* (Lidor et al., 2001) identified Dr Crocker as one of the top three sport psychology researchers in Canada.

Csikszentmihalyi, Mihaly. Hungarian psychology professor.

Dalton, Katharina (1916–2004). British gynaecologist and pioneer in the research of premenstrual stress syndrome.

Da Vinci, Leonardo (1452–1519). Italian polymath, painter, sculptor, architect, musician, mathematician, engineer, inventor, anatomist, geologist, cartographer, botanist and writer.

Dawson, Karl. EFT founding master and creator of Matrix Reimprinting and co-author of the Hay House book *Matrix Reimprinting using EFT* released in August 2010.

'Desiderata'. A 1927 prose poem by American writer Max Ehrmann.

Diana, Princess of Wales (1961–1997). Born Lady Diana Frances Spencer on 1 July 1961 in Norfolk. She married the Prince of Wales at St Paul's Cathedral in London on 29 July 1981. Family was very important to Princess Diana, who had two sons: Prince William and Prince Henry (Harry). After her divorce from the Prince of Wales, the Princess continued to be regarded as a member of the Royal Family. She died on Sunday, 31 August 1997 following a car crash in Paris.

Dorje, Rangjung Rigpe (1924–1981). The 16th Karmapa and spiritual leader of the Kagyu lineage of Tibetan Buddhism.

Dove, Heinrich Wilhelm (1803–1879). Prussian physicist who discovered the technique of binaural beats in 1839.

Dwyer, Kevin. Business development manager and professional speaker who chose to channel Martin Luther King on 26 October 2013.

Edison, Thomas Alva (1847–1931). American inventor and businessman whose inventions included the motion picture camera and the practical electrical light bulb.

Edwards Anthony. Security officer based in Croydon, Surrey, who chose to channel Nikola Tesla on 26 October 2013.

Einstein, Albert, (1879–1955). German born theoretical physicist.

Emotional Freedom Techniques is a form of counselling intervention that is best known through Gary Craig's *EFT Handbook*, published in late 1990s.

Emoto, Masaru (1943–2014). Japanese author, international researcher who claimed the human consciousness has an effect on the molecular structure of water. Author of *The Hidden Messages in Water*.

Epigenetics. The study of changes in gene expression or cellular phenotype, caused by mechanisms other than changes in the underlying DNA sequence. Some of these changes have been shown to be heritable.

Eriksson, Sven-Göran. Swedish football manager. Former manager of the England national football team.

Fiennes OBE, Ranulph (b. 7 March 1944). An English adventurer and holder of several endurance records. He was the first person to visit both the north and south poles by surface means and the first to completely cross Antarctica on foot.

'Flexible working and performance', April 2008. This report details the findings of the two year research project conducted by Cranfield School of Management and Working Families into the impact of flexible working practices on employee performance. Seven leading companies took part in the research: Centrica, Citi, KPMG, Lehman Brothers, Microsoft, Pfizer and the Defence Aerospace business in Rolls Royce.

For further information on the research contact Dr Clare Kelliher at the Cranfield School of Management.

Freud, Sigmund (1856–1939). Austrian neurologist who is credited as the founding father of psychoanalysis.

Gandhi, Mohandas Karamchand (1869–1948). Led India to independence and inspired movements for civil rights globally.

Gates, Elmer R. (1859–1923). American scientist and inventor who invented the fire extinguisher and the electric iron.

Geek Squad. 24/7 tech support team for mobiles, tablets and computers operating within Carphone Warehouse.

Goodwin, Fred. Former CEO of Royal Bank of Scotland, 2001–2009.

Graves, Clare W. (1914–1986). Professor of psychology and originator of adult human development.

Gurwitsch, Alexander Gavrilovich (1874–1954). A Russian and Soviet biologist and medical scientist who originated the morphogenetic field theory and discovered the biophoton.

Hamilton PhD, David R. Has a first class honours degree in chemistry, specialising in biological and medicinal chemistry. He worked for four years in the pharmaceutical industry before becoming a bestselling author of seven books.

Haseler, Steven. Professor of politics and economics.

Hay, Louise. American motivational author, and the founder of publishing company Hay House.

Hayashi, Chujiro (1880–1940). Disciple of Mikao Usui and played a major role in the transmission of Reiki to Hawaii.

Haywood, Tony (b. 21 May 1957). British businessman and former chief executive of oil and energy company BP. His tenure ended on 1 October 2010 following the Deepwater Horizon oil spill.

Heart Breakfast. In 2010, breakfast show presenters Matt and Claire decided to do their own Big Apple Experiment™ live on Heart Radio. For seven days they shouted at their HATE apple and spoke lovingly to their LOVE apple. Nikki Owen was invited onto the show for the live on air reveal of the state of the two apples.

Heisenberg, Werner Karl (1901–1976). German theoretical physicist, Nobel Prize winner 1932 and one of the key pioneers of quantum mechanics.

Hill, Napoleon (1883–1970). American author in the area of the new thought movement. His most successful book, *Think and Grow Rich* (1937), is one of the best-selling books of all time.

House, Robert J. (1932–2011). Professor of Organisational Behaviour. The principal investigator and founder in the early 1990s of the Global Leadership and Organizational Behavior Effectiveness Research Program (GLOBE) when at the Wharton School of Business, University of Pennsylvania.

Huygens, Christiaan (1629–1695). Dutch mathematician and scientist. Published major studies of mechanics and optics.

Hyner, David. Fellow of the Professional Speakers Association (FPSA) is a renowned professional speaker who has researched how people achieve more of their potential.

Isaacs, David. Cognitive psychologist and Research Director of Chakra Institute.

Jackie (magazine). A weekly magazine for girls published by D.C. Thomsom & Co. Ltd of Dundee between 1964 and 1993.

James, Tad. Contemporary practitioner of neurolinguistic programming (NLP) and developer of Time Line Therapy™.

Jeffery, Suz. Horse whisperer who chose to channel Eleanor Roosevelt on 26 October 2013.

Jenks, Hugo. Engineer and co-creator of the experiment regarding the impact of binaural beats on apple decay.

Joan of Arc (1412–1431). French folk heroine and Catholic saint. She led the French army to several crucial victories during the Hundred Years' War, and was captured and burned at the stake by enemy forces for heresy. Her biography can be found in *The Catholic Encyclopaedia: International Work of Reference on the Constitution, Doctrine, Discipline and History of the Catholic Church*, published by Robert Appleton Company, New York in 1905.

Jobs, Steven (1955–2011). American entrepreneur and co-founder of Apple Inc.

Johnson, Boris (b. 1964). Mayor of London from 2008.

Jung, Carl Gustav (1875–1961). Swiss psychiatrist who founded analytical psychology and developed a radical new theory of the unconscious.

Karmapa, the 16th. (see Dorje, Rangjung Rigpe).

King, Justin (b. 1961). CEO of J Sainsbury plc from 2004 to 2014.

King, Martin Luther (1929–1968). American clergyman, activist and leader in the African-American Civil Rights Movement. Delivered the 'I have a Dream' speech in 1963 in Washington DC.

Kirlian photography. Photographic techniques used to capture the phenomenon of electrical coronal discharges. The technique is named after its inventor, Semyon Davidovich Kirlian, who discovered it in 1939.

Lee, Bruce (1940–1973). A Hong Kong-American martial artist, Hong Kong action film actor, martial arts instructor, philosopher and filmmaker.

Lipton, Bruce. Stem cell biologist and author of *The Biology of Belief.*

Maczka, Rick. Principal trainer at UK Centre of Excellence for NLP and Hypnotherapy Training.

Madeley, Richard and Finnigan, Judy. Husband and wife presenters of television programmes *This Morning* (1988–2001) and *Richard and Judy* (2001–2009).

Malin, Joanne. Mid-morning presenter for BBC Radio West Midlands. In 2010 Joanne did her own Big Apple Experiment™ where she revealed the apples live during an interview with Nikki Owen. As a result she backed the Big Apple Experiment™ with the belief it actually does work.

Mandel, Peter. Perfected a system called Energy Emission Analysis (EAA) for reading and interpreting Kirlian photos.

Mandela, Nelson (1918–2013). South African anti-apartheid revolutionary and politician. President of South Africa 1994–1999.

Maslow, Abraham (1908–1970). American psychologist. He developed the theory of human motivation now known as Maslow's hierarchy of needs.

Matthews, Paul. MD and founder of People Alchemy. Speaker, author and consultant on performance, capability and informal learning who observed and gave feedback to members of the channelling session on 26 October 2013.

Maxwell, Ian Robert (1923–1991). Publisher.

McCartney MBE, Sir Paul (b. 18 June 1942). An English singer-songwriter, multi-instrumentalist and composer. He gained worldwide fame as a member of The Beatles before pursuing a solo career.

McKenna, Paul (b. 1963). English hypnotist and author of self-help books.

Miller, George (1920–2012). One of the founders of the cognitive psychology field. He worked for the following institutions: American Psychological Association, Harvard University, Massachusetts Institute of Technology, Oxford University, Princeton University, Rockefeller University, University of Alabama. Alma mater: Harvard University, University of Alabama.

Mitchell, Edgar. Retired captain in the United States Navy and NASA astronaut.

Molero, Fernando. Researcher in charisma and transformational leadership.

Monroe, Marilyn born Norma Jeane Mortenson (June 1926–August 1962). An American actress, model and singer, who became a major sex symbol during the 1950s and early 1960s.

Murray, Andy (b. 15 May 1987). Scottish professional tennis player, ranked amongst the world's top players.

National Academy of Sciences. A non-profit organisation in the United States. Members serve pro bono as 'advisers to the nation on science, engineering, and medicine'.

Nefertiti, Neferneferuaten (c.1370–c.1330 BC). The Great Royal Wife (chief consort) of Akhenaten, an Egyptian Pharaoh.

Nicholson, Vivian (b. 1936). Became publicly known overnight in 1961 when her husband won £152,319 (equivalent to nearly 3 million pounds in 2015) and she announced that she would 'spend, spend, spend'.

Noetic science. The Institute of Noetic Sciences, founded in 1973 by Apollo 14 astronaut Edgar Mitchell, is a non-profit research, education and membership organisation whose mission is supporting individual and collective transformation through consciousness research, educational outreach and engaging a global learning community in the realisation of our human potential.

Obama, Barack Hussein. 44th President of the United States; assumed office 20 January 2009.

Oster, Dr Gerald. Biophysicist who in 1973 presented a paper 'Auditory beats in the brain' in the *Scientific American* that sparked further research into binaural beats.

Peron, Eva (1919–1952). First Lady of Argentina from 1946 until her death.

Porges, Stephen. Professor in the Department of Psychiatry and the director of the Brain-Body Center in the College of Medicine at the University of Illinois, Chicago.

Presley, Elvis (1935–1977). American singer, musician and actor.

Princeton's Engineering Anomalies Research (PEAR) programme, which flourished for nearly three decades under the aegis of Princeton University's School of Engineering and Applied Science, has completed its experimental agenda of studying the interaction of human consciousness.

Quantum physics, also known as quantum mechanics and quantum theory, is a fundamental branch of physics which deals with physical phenomena at nanoscopic scales that explains the behaviour of matter and its interactions with energy on the scale of atoms and subatomic particles.

Railo, Willi (1941–2010). Norwegian sport psychologist and professor of performance psychology.

Reticular activating system (RAS). A set of connected nuclei in the brains of vertebrates that is responsible for regulating arousal to certain stimuli based on what is important to you or what you have been programmed to notice. Also known as the extrathalamic control modulatory system.

Richards, Jessica. Personal transformation specialist, author and hypnotherapist who channelled Neferneferuaten Nefertiti on 26 October 2013.

Roosevelt, Anna Eleanor (1884–1962). Longest serving First Lady of the United States.

Saldanha, Jacintha. British nurse who worked at King Edward VII's Hospital Sister Agnes. On 7 December 2012 she was found dead by apparent suicide three days after falling for a prank phone call as part of a radio stunt.

Schulze, Richard M. Founder and past chairman of Best Buy.

Schwartz, Gary E. PhD. Professor of psychology, medicine, neurology, psychiatry and surgery at the University of Arizona, Director of Laboratory for Advances in Consciousness and Health and Corporate Director of Development of Healing Energy for the Canyon Ranch Resorts.

Shils, Edward (1910–1995). American sociologist.

Skinner, Sue (BSc Hons Anthropology from University College of London). A family friend since 1985. She is a Buddhist and a Reiki Master. Sue studies how new science impinges on spirituality and health and is particularly interested in Sufism, Buddhism, Hinduism and getting back to the Aramaic teachings of Jesus.

Spence, Gerry. Actual name Gerald Leonard 'Gerry' Spence. American trial lawyer.

Sperry, Roger W. (1913–1994). American neuropsychologist, neurobiologist and Nobel laureate who conducted split brain experiments.

Streep, Meryl (b. 1949). Award winning American actress.

Szent-Gyorgyi, Albert (1893–1986). Hungarian physiologist who won the Nobel Prize in Physiology or Medicine in 1937, and author of *Theory of Syntropy and Creationism* in association with Jerry Bergman, PhD, 1977.

Takata, Hawayo Hiromi (1900–1980). Introduced the spiritual practice of Reiki to the western world.

Tesla, Nikola (1856–1943). Serbian-American inventor, electrical engineer, mechanical engineer, physicist and futurist known for his contributions to the design of the modern alternating current (AC) electricity supply system.

Thatcher, Margaret (1925–2013). British Prime Minister 1979–1990; Leader of the Conservative Party 1975–1990.

The Dark Charisma of Adolf Hitler. Three-part TV mini-series first shown in 2012 on BBC Two.

'The Truth about Personality'. A *Horizon* documentary with Michael Mosley first aired on BBC Two on 11 July 2013.

The Wright Stuff, Channel Five.

Tickner, Angela. MCIPD professional trainer, facilitator and coach who chose to channel Winston Churchill on 26 October 2013.

Tickner, John. Licensed aircraft engineer and consultant who attended Nikki Owen's charisma seminar at Shakespeare's Globe Theatre in September 2012. He provided an interesting perspective on how dowsing works and his theory for why the Big Apple Experiment™ works.

Tickner, Richard (Ted). Business coach and trainer who chose to channel Gandhi on 26 October 2013.

Transcript of the BBC One Panorama interview with the Princess of Wales, interviewed by Martin Bashir, broadcast in November 1995. http://www.bbc.co.uk/news/special/politics97/diana/panorama.html

Transworld Publishers Inc. British publishing division of Random House and belongs to Bertelsmann, one of the world's largest media groups.

Twain, Mark. 'Anger is an acid that can do more harm to the vessel in which it is stored than to anything on which it is poured.' Subsequently paraphrased by Gandhi.

Usui, Mikao (1865–1926). Founder of Reiki, a form of spiritual practice.

Van den Brink, Dolf. President and chief executive of Heineken USA.

Vitruvian Man. Drawing by Leonardo da Vinci *c.*1490 accompanied by notes kept in the Gallerie dell'Accademia, Venice, Italy, reference 228.

Walsch, Neal Donald. American author of the series Conversations with God.

Wayman, Paul. Psychic medium, hypnotherapist and past life therapist.

Weber, Max (1864–1920). German socialist, philosopher and political economist.

Wharton, Mark (b. 1959). Personal breakthrough coach who chose to channel Leonardo da Vinci on 26 October 2013.

Williams, Robbie (b. 1974). Singer and composer.

Williams, Robin (1951–2014). American actor and comedian.

Bibliography

Albom, M. (2004). *The Five People You Meet in Heaven*. Sphere

Alessandra, T. (2000). *Charisma: Seven Keys to Developing the Magnetism That Leads to Success*. Warner Business Books, p. 11

Antonakis, J., Fenley, M. and Liechti, S. (2011). 'Can charisma be taught? Tests of two interventions'. Academy of Management Learning and Education, University of Lausanne

Antonakis, J., Fenley, M. and Liechti, S. (2012). 'Learning charisma'. *Harvard Business Review*

Bacon, F. Sir (2010). *Meditationes Sacrae and Human Philosophy*. Kessinger Publishing

Bastin, S. and Henken, K. (1997). 'Water content of fruits and vegetables'. http://www2.ca.uky.edu/enri/pubs/enri129.pdf

Bono, J.E. and Ilies, R. (2006). 'Charisma, positive emotions and mood contagion'. *The Leadership Quarterly*, 17

Brown, E. (2010). *Dowsing – The Ultimate Guide for the 21st Century*. Hay House

Brown, G. (2010). 'Gordon Brown's resignation speech in full'. *The Guardian*, 11 May

Burnett, F.H. (1911). *The Secret Garden*. Heinemann

Byrne, R. (2006). *The Secret*. Atria

Cabane, O.F. (2012). *The Charisma Myth*. Portfolio

Calaprice, A. (2005). *The New Quotable Einstein*. Princeton University Press, p. 206

CBI (2014). 'Growth for everyone: CBI/Accenture employment trends survey 2014'. CBI

CBS (2007). 'Eye To Eye: Richard Branson (CBS News)'. http://www.youtube.com/watch?v=Q6hILGfbqSg&feature=fvw 31 July

Chamorro-Premuzic, T. (2012). 'The dark side of charisma'. *Harvard Business Review*, 16 November

Church, D. (2008). *The Genie in Your Genes*. Energy Psychology Press

CIPD and Simplyhealth (2012). 'Absence management 2012'. CIPD and Simplyhealth

Coffman, C. (2002). Interviewed by Barb Sanford in 'The high cost of disengaged employees'. Gallup Business Journal, 15 April

Csiksgentmihalyi, M. (2002). *Flow: The Psychology of Happiness*. Rider

Dawson, K. and Allenby, S. (2010). *Matrix Reimprinting using EFT*. Hay House

De Cremer, D. and van Knippenberg, D. (2002). 'How do leaders promote cooperation? The effects of charisma and procedural fairness'. *Journal of Applied Psychology*, 87(5), 858–866

Einstein, A. and Infeld, L. (1938). *The Evolution of Physics*. Cambridge University Press

Eisenstadt, S.N. (1968). *Max Weber on Charisma and Institution Building*. University of Chicago

Emoto, M. (2005). *The Hidden Messages in Water*. Atria Books

Flook, R. with van Overbruggen, R. (2009). *Why Am I Sick?* BookSurge Publishing

Gladwell, M. (2009). *Outliers: The Story of Success*. Penguin

Grant, A., Gino, F. and Hofma, D.A. (2010). 'The hidden advantages of quiet bosses'. *Harvard Business Review*

Graves, Clare W. (1970). 'Levels of existence: an open system theory of values'. *Journal of Humanistic Psychology*, November

Halberstadt, J. (2010). 'Intuition: dumb but lucky. Fortuitous affective cues and their disruption by analytic thought'. onlinelibrary.wiley.com

Hay, L. (2004). You Can Heal Your Life. Hay House

Hay Group (2012). 'Depressed employee engagement stunts global business performance'. Hay Group Insight Report, 13 November

Hayward, T. (2010). 'I want my life back'. Available at http://archive.fortune.com/2010/06/10/news/companies/tony_hayward_quotes.fortune/index.htm 31 May

Hill, N. (1953). *Think and Grow Rich*. Ralston Publishing Company. Originally published in 1937

Institute of Noetic Sciences (n.d.) 'IONS' Pioneering Work on "Distant Healing" Suggests Further Study Warranted'. http://www.noetic.org/about/case-studies/love-study/

International Labour Organization (2011). *Global Employment Trends 2011*. International Labour Organization

Jung, C.G. (1964). *Man and His Symbols*. Doubleday

Kline, N. (1999). *Time to Think*. Cassell

Lee, B. (2001). *Bruce Lee: Artist of Life. Edited by John Little*. Tuttle Publishing

Lidor, R., Morris, T., Bardaxoglu, N. and Becker Jr, B. (2001). *World Sport Psychology*. Fitness Information Technology, Inc.

Lipton, B.H. (2005). *The Biology of Belief*. Hay House, Inc.

Living, J. (2008). *Institution Technology*. The Holistic Intuition Society

Mainwaring, S. (2012). 'President Clinton's ability to scale intimacy'. Available at: forbes.com 11 September

Maltz, M. (1960). *Psycho-cybernetics*. Prentice-Hall, Inc.

Mandel, P. (1993). *Esogetics: The Sense and Nonsense of Sickness and Pain*. Energetik Verlag GmbH

Mandela, N. (2012). *Notes to the Future: Words of Wisdom*. Simon and Schuster

Maslow, A. (1943). 'A theory of human motivation'. *Psychological Review*

Mayer, J.D. and Salovey, P. (1997). 'What is emotional intelligence?', in Salovey, P. and Sluyter, D. (eds), *Emotional Development and Emotional Intelligence: Implications for Educators*. Basic Books

Mayer, J.D., Salovey, P. and Caruso, D.R. (2004). 'Emotional intelligence: theory, findings, and implications'. *Psychological Inquiry*

McTaggart, L. (2001). *The Field*. Element

McTaggart, L. (2007). *The Intention Experiment*. HarperElement

Miller, G.A. (1956). 'Magical number seven, plus or minus two: some limits on our capacity for processing' (Miller's Law). *Psychological Review*

Molero, F. (1995). 'The study of charisma and charismatic leadership in social sciences: a psychosocial approach'. *International Journal of Social Psychology*, 10(1)

Molero, F., Cuadrado, I., Navas, M. and Morales, J.F. (2007). 'Relations and effects of transformational leadership: a comparative analysis with traditional leadership styles'. *The Spanish Journal of Psychology*, 10(2)

Nicholas, S. (2010). 'Could talking to an apple help you become more beautiful?' *Daily Mail*, 15 March

Nixon, L. (2009). *Discover the DNA of Future CEOs*. The Korn Ferry Institute, December

O'Boyle, E. (2012). Interviewed by Gallup in 'The business impact of human emotions'. Gallup Business Journal, 1 November

Oschman, J.L. (2000). *Energy Medicine: The Scientific Basis*. Elsevier Limited

Owen, N. (1992). *Nicola – A Second Chance to Live*. Transworld Publishing

Owen, N. (2008). 'Releasing your hidden charisma'. Businessballs

Owen, N. and Miller, A. (2004). 'The five most dangerous issues facing sales leaders today and how to guarantee a permanent improvement in sales results'. Businessballs, businessballs.com/trainiquesalesresearch.pdf

Pearce, E.C. (1975). *Anatomy and Physiology for Nurses: Including Notes on Their Clinical Application*. Faber

Pearsall, P. (1998). *The Heart's Code*. Thorsons

Pennington, J.A.T. and Spungen, J.S. (2009). *Bowes and Church's Food Values of Portions Commonly Used*. LWW

Porges, S.W. (2010). 'Early development of the autonomic nervous system'. Brain-Body Centre, University of Illinois, Chicago

Porges, S.W. (2011). *The Polyvagal Theory: Neurophysical Foundations of Emotions, Attachment, Communication and Self-Regulation*. W.W. Norton & Company

Redfield, J. (1994). *The Celestine Prophecy*. Bantam

Reed, H. (1989). *Edgar Cayce on Channeling Your Higher Self*. Warner Books

Riley-Smith, B. (2013). 'The wit and wisdom of Prince Charles'. *The Telegraph*, 14 November

Salovey, P., Rothmans, A.J., Detweiler, J.B. and Steward, W.T. (2000). 'Emotional states and physical health'. *American Psychologist*, January

Sankowsky, D. (1995). *The Charismatic Leader as Narcissist: Understanding the Abuse of Power*. Elsevier Inc.

Schiuma, G., Mason, S. and Kennerley, M. (2006). 'UK Business loses productivity through poor workforce energy management'. Lucozade Energy and the Centre for Business Performance, Cranfield School of Management, 30 October

Shils, E. (1965). 'Charisma, order, and status'. *American Sociological Review*, 30(2)

Shils, E. (1991). *The Constitution of Society*. University of Chicago Press

Sicher, F., Targ, E., Moore II, D. and Smith, H. (1998). 'A randomized double-blind study of the effect of distant healing in a population with advanced AIDS'. *Western Journal of Medicine*, 169(6), 356–363

Sinek, S. (2014). *Leaders Eat Last: Why Some Teams Pull Together and Others Don't*. Portfolio

Smith, C.R. (2000). *Quest for Charisma: Christianity and Persuasion*. Praeger Publishers

Spence, G. (2008). *How to Argue and Win Every Time*. St. Martin's Press Reprint

Sturgess, S. (2014). *The Book of Chakras & Subtle Bodies*. Watkins Publishing Limited

Syed, M. (2010). *Bounce – How Champions are Made*. Fourth Estate

Tasler, N. (2002). 'Five secrets of charismatic leadership'. Bloomberg Business, November

Wallace, B.A. (2004). *The Taboo of Subjectivity – Toward a New Science of Consciousness*. Oxford Scholarship Online

Weber, M.S. (2000). *Wirtschaft und Gesellschaft – Grundrib der verstehenden Soziologie*. Mohr Siebeck

Willey, R.C. (1984). *Modern Dowsing*. Treasure Chest Publications

About the author

Nikki Owen is an award winning and international speaker on charismatic leadership. When she was eighteen she experienced the charisma of a leader who transformed her own life against all the odds. This event compelled her to dedicate over twenty years to researching and studying charisma. She is justifiably a world expert. Nikki has a generosity of spirit and a belief that every individual possesses the power to change their world. Thousands of business leaders have experienced her ability to change their lives using her unique approach. Nikki lives in the Kent countryside.

For more information about Nikki's work on charisma you can email her at nikkiowen@audiencewithcharisma.com or visit www.nikkijowen.com